COMMUNICATING BEYOND LANGUAGE

Communicating Beyond Language offers a timely and lively appraisal of the concept of communicative repertoires—resources we use to express who we are when in dialogue with others. Each chapter describes and illustrates the communicative resources humans deploy daily, but rarely think about—not only the multiple languages we use, but how we dress or gesture, how we greet each other or tell stories, the nicknames we coin, and the mass-media references we make—and how these resources combine in infinitely varied performances of identity. The book also discusses how our repertoires shift and grow over the course of a lifetime, as well as how a repertoire perspective can lead to a rethinking of cultural diversity and human interaction, from categorizing people's differences to understanding how our repertoires can expand and overlap with others', thereby helping us to find common ground and communicate in increasingly multicultural schools, workplaces, markets, and social spheres.

This book affirms the importance of communicative repertoires with highly engaging discussions and contemporary examples from mass media, popular culture, and everyday life. The result is a fresh and exciting work that will resonate with students and scholars in sociolinguistics, intercultural communication, applied linguistics, and education.

Betsy Rymes is Associate Professor of Educational Linguistics at the Graduate School of Education at the University of Pennsylvania.

COMMUNICATING BEYOND LANGUAGE

Everyday Encounters with Diversity

Betsy Rymes

Routledge
Taylor & Francis Group

NEW YORK AND LONDON

First published 2014
by Routledge
711 Third Avenue, New York, NY 10017

and by Routledge
2 Park Square, Milton Park, Abingdon, Oxon OX14 4RN

Routledge is an imprint of the Taylor & Francis Group, an informa business

© 2014 Taylor & Francis

Library of Congress Cataloging in Publication Data
Rymes, Betsy.
Communicating beyond language : everyday encounters with diversity / Betsy R. Rymes, University of Pennsylvania.
  pages cm
Includes bibliographical references and index.
1. Communication—Social aspects.
2. Interpersonal communication—Social aspects. 3. Rhetoric—Social aspects.
4. Discourse analysis—Social aspects. 5. Multilingualism—Social aspects.
6. Language and languages—Variation. 7. Communication and culture.
8. Sociolinguistics. I. Title.
P95.54.R96 2014
302.2—dc23
2013023751

ISBN: 978–0–415–50338–9 (hbk)
ISBN: 978–0–415–50340–2 (pbk)
ISBN: 978–0–203–12961–6 (ebk)

Typeset in Bembo
by Swales & Willis Ltd, Exeter, Devon

Printed in Great Britain by TJ International Ltd, Padstow, Cornwall

CONTENTS

ILLUSTRATIONS

Figures

Tables

ACKNOWLEDGMENTS

As this book has illustrated (or will, if you have yet to read it!), an individual's communicative repertoire grows out of life's accumulation of interactions and experiences. Likewise, my writing of this book has come to fruition in large part through the conversations, discussions, and arguments, far flung experiences, and marginal comments that have contributed to my communicative repertoire over the years.

Countless ideas and interactions are represented within the pages of this book only because of the generosity, open spirit, and overall magnanimous and gifted teaching presence of Robert Zakrzewsky (aka Mr. Z). His enthusiasm for the repertoire range of his students and his willingness to include me and many graduate students in his classroom community over several years has been a formative part of my own and my students' understandings of contemporary urban vernaculars in Philadelphia and their impact on classroom life.

Many formative discussions have happened right here at Penn. I am indebted to the generosity of my colleagues here for providing me opportunities to present my ideas—at various stages—to a widely varying and universally super-smart audience of faculty and graduate students. In particular I thank Nancy Hornberger for the fortitude she brings to sustaining structures for intellectual exchange and for encouraging dialogue among faculty and students. Our signature Proseminars and the lively discussions they have sparked have been an invaluable source of ideas, intellectual sustenance, and encouragement for me. I thank those at Penn who have generously contributed questions and ideas and expanded my repertoire. Among that group my former colleague and forever friend, Kathy Howard, deserves special mention. Also going above and beyond intellectual exchange, Anne Pomerantz, Nelson Flores, and Robert Moore have especially and unfailingly been sources of insight, new ideas, and hilarity that daily make working and thinking about communication more lively and intense. And, Stanton Wortham's support in all matters, from the mundane to the momentous, has, consistently, over the years, helped me to develop many of the ideas presented here.

Students have also made vast contributions to my repertoire. They have not only been takers of fieldnotes, compressors of video, tireless transcribers, and patient organizers—they have also, through their own research and insights, and countless discussions in my office and our classrooms, profoundly inspired me, influenced my thinking, and been a source of endless examples of phenomena discussed here. In particular I thank Geeta Aneja, Catrice Barrett, Sofia Chaparro, Mariam Durani, Sarah Gallo, Heather Hurst, Holly Link, Jackie Lopez, Joanna Siegel, Krystal Smalls, and Karl Swinehart.

Discussions among colleagues and students have also led to conversations further afield. I thank Maureen Matarese for inviting me to first present ideas on metacommentary at the International Linguistic Association Conference in New York; to Doris Wariner for inviting me to present many of the materials that are in Chapter 5, on Storytelling, and to James Wilce and Anna De Fina for their generous comments on some of those ideas. I am forever grateful to Sandro Duranti for both his model as a scholar and for inviting me to present much of the material in Chapter 4, on Mass Media, in Los Angeles at UCLA's Center for Language Interaction and Culture. Chapter 4 has benefited from the critique I received there from the generous audience members including my mentor, Elinor Ochs, as well as Steve Clayman, and John Heritage. I also owe endless thanks to my editors, Leah Babb-Rosenfield and Elysse Preposi, for providing the opportunity to collect my ideas into a book and for their patience and encouragement as it came together. Many thanks, also, to the anonymous reviewers whose critiques provided a springboard for new ideas.

Far from my current home, but close to my heart, I thank my mother, Gretchen Kreuter, and my father, Kent Kreuter, for a lifetime of unconditional, yet critical, encouragement to pursue whatever I seem to be ranting on about. They have given me the courage to pursue new ideas, to foster creativity in my students and my children, and to know that the value of new generations is not simply to repeat whatever the older generations have done, said, and believed, but to add something new.

Back to home: My children, Charlie and Anya, who possess endlessly fascinating and ephemeral communicative repertoires, have daily opened my eyes to the vast ranges of potential joy, humor, and intensity in every interaction. Charlie has given me sage advice on countless speech acts ("Dance with me, you pretty, sweet fool!") that I have tested on him ("Mom, you just should never say that."). He also, wisely, advised me against using a piñata metaphor to structure this acknowledgments section. And Anya has entertained us endlessly with her own repertoire experimentation and metacommentary ("Psych!—Wait, what does psych mean?"). Despite their generous contributions and input, please don't blame my children, or anyone else mentioned here for any flaws or embarrassments that remain in this book. And, if my brief foray into my own communicative repertoire has missed some contributors—apologies in advance! I will remember you gratefully when, in time, I hear and recognize your words in my own.

Betsy Rymes
Philadelphia, June 2013

1

A REPERTOIRE APPROACH

Take a walk today down a street in any large urban center, anywhere in the world, and you will encounter multiple ways of speaking and dressing, gesturing and greeting, expressing sadness or joy, love or hate—in short, massive communicative diversity. How do we learn to get along in this complex communicative milieu? How do people who walk down the same street and who share a common humanity but express themselves radically differently live together without continual conflict and chaos? This book addresses these questions by describing the *communicative repertoires* through which, in dialogue with others, we express who we are and find common ground. Each chapter describes and illustrates communicative resources humans deploy daily, but rarely think about—not only the multiple languages we use, but how we dress or gesture, how we greet each other or tell stories, the names and nicknames we coin, the mass media references we make—and how these resources combine in infinitely varied ways when people interact.

Often, these interactional combinations happen in multiple languages and, always, in concert with expressive creativity that goes "beyond language." Below, I elucidate what I mean by "communicating beyond language" piece-by-piece— defining in abstract brevity what the rest of the book will elaborate and exemplify. Then I will briefly explain two critical analytic pathways to examining such communicating: First, I use the concept of *communicative repertoire* to draw our attention to the multiplicity of communicative means. Second, I use the concept of *everyday metacommentary* (commenting on communication) to illuminate which features of one's repertoire are most relevant. In exemplifying different forms of "communicating beyond language," or, as described in the subtitle of this book, "everyday encounters with diversity," I will return to these concepts of *communicative repertoire* and *metacommentary* throughout the volume.

Communicating

What counts as "communicating"? Engaging a teenager in a conversation about sex? Writing a paper for a graduate school seminar? Using spoken Hindi in a high school English class? This book illustrates how each of these scenarios potentially counts as communicating but some may be more mutually engaging, depending on how people approach each other. Over the course of a lifetime, as humans move in and out of vastly varying contexts of social relations, communicating requires massive flexibility: A parent of young teens is surprised to realize she knows that the phrase "sick" is a positive modifier; a graduate student suddenly impresses herself by using the word "alterity" having never learned an explicit definition; a high-school student born and raised in Philadelphia starts ironically using the Bollywood/Hindi term of endearment "*Jaan-e-man*" (sweetheart) when talking with his South Asian-American classmates. In each of these cases, people's repertoires are expanding to overlap with those of their family, friends, classmates or colleagues. In this way, they are communicating.

Every day, students in most urban schools face these kinds of communicative complexities. As soon as students enter any public school in the United States they are, by law, given a home language survey. It is not uncommon for a single urban high school to collect home language surveys reporting over 75 home languages. And, in many homes, far more than a single language is called on to communicate. Individual students who come from those homes are usually multilingual themselves. As one Moroccan ninth-grader in a Philadelphia area high school explained to me, "At home, we speak English, French, Spanish, Arabic, a little of it all." Usually, this multilingualism is not restricted to "home": Another student from the same school speaks a little Urdu/Hindi, Pashto, and English all evening in his after-school job at a family store. Another speaks French and English at a hair-braiding shop where she works. These students need each of these languages in order to communicate in different contexts, every day.

Beyond Language

So, with all these languages in circulation, why talk about communication *beyond* language? Each of the examples above illustrates the multiplicity of languages— French, English, Arabic, Hindi—people use. What other forms of communication do we learn as we enter a new community? As the parents of kids who use "sick" as a complement witness, these kids may also have very specific ways of acting when they say "sick!"—as well as specific clothes they wear and things they carry. The same holds true for a high school friend calling out "Jaan-e-man" or a graduate student mentioning "alterity," who most likely is wearing jeans and an old t-shirt and carrying a backpack.

Similarly, as multilingual students begin to navigate school, they will need to call on a communicative repertoire that extends beyond those represented by language labels given on the home language survey. How they dress, what their hair looks like, the nicknames they go by, how they greet, say goodbye, express thanks, respond to teacher questions, format an essay, or invite a friend home with them, will all influence their pathway through school and life. This book emphasizes this entire repertoire of communicative tools as a way of understanding not only how a multilingual teenager navigates high school, but how, in this massively diversifying world, accomplishing even basic daily routines requires greater awareness of those forms of communicative diversity that, while often below our conscious awareness, are crucial to successful interaction.

Building Common Ground: Comembership and Participatory Culture

All the scenarios given so far also illustrate another point about communicating: It involves more than one person. I do not communicate to someone, *we communicate* together. This should be obvious. However, much of language instruction is based on a notion of "correctness" that entails individual—not collaborative—mastery. Once an individual "internalizes" a set of rules, that individual will be able to spew out correct language. Many people can take years of language classes and score well on language proficiency tests, but have extreme difficulty communicating in that language. And yet, most of the time, people are concerned with communicating to one another, not achieving a perfect language test score. Accordingly, this book illustrates how people communicate collaboratively, in interaction: At times seeking out those areas of overlap that can lead to fulfilling engagements with other people; at other times, running into communicative blocks.

Starting from the point of view that communicating is a collaborative activity, this book builds from interactional sociolinguistic and anthropological models of communication (rather than strictly linguistic ones) as useful ways to understand interaction, because such models are grounded in what people do *with each other*. Those who study social interaction and learning have looked carefully at how people seek out common ground, even in cases where languages are not completely shared or differences seem, initially, to be prohibitive of successful communication.

So, if individuals' proficiency in a shared language is not the sufficient common ground to hold us together as communicators, what else is needed? What sustains interaction and encourages people to share themselves? What gives us the sense we will be understood? To answer this question, Fred Erickson and Jeff Shultz (1982), carefully analyzed the negotiation of common ground in the context of college counselor and student meetings—what they call "gate-keeping interviews." While all the participants were speakers of English, the counselor and the various college students differed from each other in many obvious ways. So, part of the interactional work in these sessions involved figuring out how to communicate across those differences. Finding common ground was crucial in these interviews and this exploration occurred through initial negotiation of "comembership" which Erickson and Shultz (p. 17) defined as follows:

> Comembership is an aspect of performed social identity that involves particularistic attributes of status shared by counselor and student—for example, race and ethnicity, sex, interest in football, graduation from the same high school, acquaintance with the same individual.

While the obvious demographic segmentations "race, ethnicity, sex" are involved as candidate comembership categories, Erickson and Shultz emphasize that there was far more fluidity in what could evolve into comembership. And whatever became the grounds for comembership, when participants in a counseling interaction shared high degrees of comembership, the counselor aligned with the interests of the student. However, when some degree of comembership was not arrived at, the counselor aligned with the institution. This research also made it clear that alignment during an interaction was contingent more on extra-linguistic cues—such as body language, gestures, and intonation—than on language itself or even the content of what was being said. Arriving at comembership was less like an exchange of information than a dance, a *pas de deux* in which each partner carefully negotiated with the other physically and emotionally to arrive at a shared sense of order.

Erickson and Shultz's work on comembership introduced the notion that communication is a careful negotiation about what those communicating share and how that common ground can build through an interaction—even a highly controlled interaction like an advising session, in which the advisee and the advisor are being pushed together artificially by extrinsic, institutional concerns.

But what about situations where people do not need to interact? What draws people together—even people who might not seem very much alike—to start communicating? Sometimes "comembership" around a common cause such as a video game (*World of Warcraft*), a popular book (*Harry Potter*), or a hobby (beer making) is enough to bring otherwise widely divergent types of people together. Gee describes "affinity spaces" as just such phenomena, defining them as "real world or internet sites or virtual worlds like Second Life—where people interact around a common passion" (Hayes & Gee, 2010). Affinity spaces find their cohesion through something like what Erickson and Shultz called "comembership" with the usual race/class/gender identity categories slipping even more to the background: "In an affinity space, people relate to each other primarily in terms of common interests, endeavors, goals, or practices, not primarily in terms of race, gender, age, disability, or social class" (Hayes & Gee, 2010, p. 188).

In addition, affinity spaces are places where highly diverse forms of knowledge converge: "Affinity space encourages and enables people to use dispersed knowledge, knowledge that is not actually at the site itself, but at other sites."

So, for Gee, affinity spaces offer ideal sites for learning because individuals pool knowledge that is not shared, negotiating overlap and relevance. Participants are motivated to communicate with each other because they want to learn more about the common interest. In these spaces, even language(s) are often pooled, as when fan-fiction writers use a medley of Japanese, Chinese, and English to convey character and flair in their fiction writing (Black, 2008).

So people are drawn together and motivated to communicate through comembership and shared affinities. As Erickson and Shultz found, counselors align with students' concerns when they share common ground. As Gee and others have illustrated, once participants in affinity spaces find each other, they also welcome new knowledge into the space, building more common ground. Are these features of communication unique to internet spaces or counseling sessions? Or are these phenomena illustrating something more general about communication and culture?

Henry Jenkins (2006) argues that this collective form of knowledge building is characteristic of late-modern society and has dubbed this form of communication *participatory culture*. In lieu of other, more traditional, organized groups like nation states or a grade in school (Class of 2012!), participatory culture develops among people with shared interests or goals—such as *Star Wars* fans, PhD students working on their dissertations, skateboarding-video-makers or people contributing to Wikipedia. Within participatory culture, knowledge and authority are loosely negotiated and even what the group is about can change as members themselves assert changing priorities.

Wikipedia offers an illustration of how participatory culture works: Jimmy Wales, the founder of Wikipedia, has created an infrastructure, but he has very little role in determining the content of the site. The entries that emerge, the information that is in those entries, and the quality and modality of those entries is all determined via voluntary collaboration of the Wikipedia users and producers. What Wikipedia ends up being is a result of participatory culture of those who contribute to it. In participatory culture, the canon of important knowledge is not decided on by an isolated elite, but negotiated among people who are involved in the world, as they express what they already know and what they care about knowing more of.

Drawing on Levy's (1997) notion of *Collective Intelligence*, Jenkins (2006) links "the emergence of the new knowledge space [in participatory culture] to the breakdown of geographic constraints on communication, of the declining loyalty of individuals to organized groups, and of the diminished power of nation states to command the exclusive loyalty of their citizens" (p. 137). Through participatory culture, loyalty or popularity or even legitimacy is not received on demand or through a top-down power structure, but earned by providing something creative or new, but still of shared interest to the group.

So, the basic interactional features of comembership, carefully described by Erickson and Shultz, and the "affinity spaces" and "participatory culture" described by Gee and Jenkins all illustrate features of communication that are inherently and necessarily collective—and, perhaps, characteristic of our late-modern world. Arriving at the right ways of speaking or the important knowledge does not happen through unilateral effort or institutional authority. Rather, people in interaction collaboratively negotiate what counts as knowledge and what are the functional resources for communicating.

The processes of negotiating comembership, entering an affinity space, or engaging in participatory culture, illustrate how individuals find common ground by simultaneously building on commonalities (e.g., common goals for a Wikipedia entry) and by tapping into each other's diverse backgrounds (e.g., knowledge to create different Wikipedia entries). Moreover, the extent to which people find those points of commonality indicates the extent to which they can communicate with each across other points of difference—building on each other's *communicative repertoires* while expanding their own.

A Repertoire Approach

Whether in an academic counseling session, on a fan-fiction chat site, or by enhancing a Wikipedia entry, individuals communicate across difference by negotiating or seeking out common ground and, then, creating new shared terrain. To investigate this process of finding common ground in more detail, this book takes a *repertoire approach*. I call an individual's resource set a *communicative repertoire*. The extent to which we can communicate is contingent on the degree to which our repertoires expand, change and overlap with others.

As Erickson and Shultz's close analysis of talk illustrates, people form alignments in interaction not necessarily by speaking the same native language (e.g., "English" or "Spanish") or categorizing each other demographically, but when they find some kind of common ground. In this sense, we learn to live side-by-side by expanding our communicative repertoires. As our repertoire gradually shifts to overlap with that of others (including common ways of greeting, joking, gesturing or dressing, for example) we develop a sense of shared belonging. This perspective should lead to rethinking how we encounter "cultural diversity" in any setting—the workplace, a classroom, a family, a neighborhood market, or a local park. Understanding "the other" is not a matter of labeling and demarcating that person's differences in potentially essentializing or stereotypical ways, but of raising awareness of multiple repertoires and expanding any potential points of communicative overlap.

A Brief History of the Repertoire Perspective

Initially, the notion of "repertoire" was a radical concept in linguistics. So, perhaps it makes sense that it emerged in the 1960s, as some linguists felt bolstered to challenge more purist orthodoxies in the interest of carefully observing social life.

During this era, John Gumperz (1964, 1965) began to question linguistic definitions of language. This questioning began when he traveled to India to do linguistic research. There, in a context of massive linguistic variety, he found that individuals habitually used many languages in seemingly free variation. They simply did not orient to the idea that languages should be used in a "pure" form. In his essay, "Language," (1965) Gumperz drew on these observations to make the point that terms like "Language X" demarcated a useful category for linguists, but not necessarily for people communicating. When the people in an Indian marketplace, for example, were bargaining with other multilingual merchants, they would strategically call on words and phrases from many different local languages to make a sale or negotiate a bargain. Gumperz's analysis of the Indian marketplace centered on language and a questioning of linguistic description, and he used the term *linguistic repertoire* to describe the range of languages circulating in a community.

Later in the 1960s and in the 1970s, Gumperz took his research even further beyond the goals of decontextualized linguistic description. Seeking to apply his methods for closely examining the nuance of negotiation—methods he developed through his research in the Indian marketplace—he began to examine emergent injustices he perceived in the interactions of Indian English speakers in London (Gumperz, 1978). While these speakers technically had become fluent in the English language, certain features of their talk—for example, intonation and emphasis—often led to miscommunication in crucial gate-keeping interactions—such as job interviews or attempts to access social services. To use the terms Erickson and Shultz coined, these simple features of communication prevented any attempts to find *comembership*—and impeded successful alignment in these high-stakes encounters.

Gumperz called the misunderstandings in these encounters, *crosstalk*, and he attributed prevalent racist attitudes in London to a cumulative build-up of these simple, yet frustrating and pervasive, interactional miscues. But was racism in London contingent on simply these audible miscues? While Gumperz made huge advances in the field of sociolinguistics by drawing attention to these micro-features of interaction that can lead to crosstalk, his analysis neglected some important features of those interactions. His earlier concept of "repertoire" included multiple languages, but he never expanded that concept to include the other features of an interaction that are beyond language—including both those that he identified in *crosstalk* as well as more general features of the context.

So, if the problem of *crosstalk* cannot be attributed exclusively to language, intonation, and stress, what other communicative elements can we hold accountable? The way someone is dressed, the color of their skin, the length of their hair, the way they sit during an interview or what kind of bag they carry their papers in, all may have an effect on how encounters with diversity unfold. Adding to the work of interactional sociolinguists, like Gumperz,

Linguistic Anthropologists have increasingly pushed the boundaries in discovering relevant communicative elements—beyond language—within interaction. As Duranti has written (1994), for example, communicating effectively in a Samoan Kava ceremony involved knowledge of a system of grammar, a range of registers, and cues about spacing and pacing of talk, but also of how seating spots were arranged, what you could wear, the ordering of events, who drank first and last, and even what a person in power should look like (large) and how they should move (slowly and not much). This kind of knowledge is a crucial component of a communicative repertoire. These are also important elements of any interaction that may have gone unanalyzed in Gumperz' more sociolinguistically focused examination of crosstalk.

So what do the Indian marketplace of the 1960s, Indian English speakers in London in the 1970s, and Samoan Kava ceremonies in the 1980s have to do with communicating in late-modern times? Today's increasingly multilingual schools and cities are in many ways analogous to the Indian marketplaces Gumperz described over 40 years ago. Gumperz' use of the term *repertoire*, the recognition that a community may contain a huge diversity of functionally relevant linguistic resources, illuminates the complex communicative needs in today's society—not simply a unique characteristic of multilingual India. As described above, most urban high schools feature dozens of home languages—and students increasingly use them with each other. Additionally, the late-modern massive "breakdown of constraints on communication"—through transnational movement and the internet—and the participatory culture it fosters (Jenkins, 2006) have led to a proliferation of multilingualism, even in monolingual strongholds like the United States. Internet communication and increased transnational movement have also meant that people moving across language boundaries are motivated to maintain languages of multiple countries—as they could be speaking with a teacher in English at one moment and Skyping with their Moroccan mother in French and Arabic the next.

Moreover, many encounters between English speakers include, like those Gumperz recorded in London in the 1970s, at least one participant for whom English is not a first language. Today, in fact, most English speakers in the world are not native speakers—outnumbering native speakers 3:1 (Crystal, 2003). Some linguists have even suggested that the "native" speakers are the ones who now risk being misunderstood unless they accommodate to the norms of other, international Englishes around them (Graddol, 1997). Given these realities, the nuances of communication that Gumperz began to describe in London are, perhaps, even more relevant to the kind of diverse encounters people have today. The conditions may also be ripe for *crosstalk* of the kind Gumperz described in 1970s' London.

So, communication today is increasingly multilingual, and like Indian English Speakers and Native Londoners, even those speaking the "same language" do so in widely varying ways. And, understanding communication these days goes beyond simply describing languages people are using. Varied expectations for routines, gestures, ways of dressing, etc., also contribute to communicative complexity. For example, while many Samoans have moved to Los Angeles and speak primarily English, some of the routines Duranti observed in Samoa in the 1980s took place many years later, in new but recognizable forms, among transnational Samoans in exurban Los Angeles (cf. Duranti & Reynolds, 2000). These routines have become part of the communicative repertoire of many transplanted Samoans. Similarly, when people communicate via the web, they have developed routines that involve photos, video, music, emoticons, and other non-linguistic forms of expression that serve as resources for communication.

In summary, multiple languages, multiple ways of speaking the "same" language, and many features beyond language can serve as part of an individual's communicative repertoire and function to create communicative alignment or *crosstalk* in interaction today. While Gumperz was using the term *linguistic repertoire* to describe the languages circulating in one community, today the use of "repertoire" has become increasingly common as a way of describing how individuals deploy other modes of communication in addition to their multiple languages.

Educational researchers have also begun to use the term "repertoire" as a way to describe the diverse forms of knowledge that students bring into the classroom. This repertoire perspective allows us to rethink classrooms as affinity spaces and sites of participatory culture rather than top-down authoritarian regimes of standardized knowledge. Imagine, for example, the variety of Wikipedia entries that could be built by a high school classroom with kids from 12 different countries and speaking as many different languages.

Once schools and classrooms are re-imagined as affinity space and sites of participatory culture, the multiple repertoires circulating in those classrooms become valuable resources rather than liabilities. Gutiérrez and Rogoff emphasize how looking at a repertoire of communicative resources (they use the phrase "repertoires of practice") allows educators to focus on the "benefits of knowing about the histories and valued practices of cultural groups rather than trying to teach prescriptively according to broad, under-examined generalities about groups" (2003, p. 20). Rather than seeing someone as different, based on race, class, gender, or country of origin, one might see points of similarity, based on other points of comembership, or shared interests of the type that develop in Gee-like affinity spaces. Rather than identifying individuals as part of one monolithic different "Culture," people can see points of commonality and shared interests, as well as the wealth of collective knowledge in a diverse classroom by contributing to a shared, "participatory culture" of that classroom.

The term *communicative repertoire* will be used throughout this volume to refer to the collection of ways individuals use language and other means of communication (gestures, dress, posture, accessories) to function effectively in the multiple communities in which they participate (Rymes, 2010). One's repertoire can include not only multiple languages, dialects, and registers in the institutionally defined sense, but also gesture, dress, posture, and even knowledge of communicative routines, familiarity with types of food or drink, and mass media references including phrases, dance moves, and recognizable intonation patterns that circulate via actors, musicians, and other superstars (Rymes, 2012). So, an individual's repertoire can be seen as something like an accumulation of archeological layers. As one moves through life, one accumulates an abundance of experiences and images, and one also selects from those experiences, choosing elements from a repertoire that seem to communicate in the moment, developing a potential for *comembership*.

The Diversity Principle

Perhaps one of the most important reasons for taking a repertoire approach is that it provides a practical pathway for engaging with diversity—as a researcher, a teacher, a student, and most basically, as a person. This is because a repertoire perspective accommodates the basic recognition that, these days, in times of massive breakdown of the usual geographic and cultural constraints, it is less useful than ever to view kinds of communication as free-standing markers of some general category type ("typical college kid … Asian … woman … Midwesterner …"). Instead, communicative elements circulate so widely these days and are taken up in such diverse ways, that it is hard to use such broad generalizations to understand what is going in.

While some communication theorists have speculated that globalization and mass media lead to homogenization of cultural elements, it turns out quite the contrary. Massive circulation of language and messages has not led to homogenization of language and communication, but to a massive diversification. This is captured in what I call "The Diversity Principle":

> **The Diversity Principle**: *The more widely circulated a communicative element is, the more highly diverse the interactions with it will be.*

To illustrate this principle in action, consider the Hindi/Urdu word *Jaan-e-man*. In a Bollywood film, the hearthrob might use this word (loosely translated, "sweetheart") to refer lovingly to his girlfriend. But now, Hindi-speaking Bollywood fans live in Philadelphia (among many other cities, globally), and in one English classroom they used it jokingly among themselves. Soon, other students (non-Hindi-speakers) began to use it too. "*Jaan-e-man*" was no longer being used as a term of endearment, like "sweetheart," but more as a way of semi-ironically getting someone's attention, as in "*Jaan-e-man*, hand me a computer." Now, given that *Jaan-e-man* and Bollywood fans have circulated across the globe via mass media and emigration, the way people use *Jaan-e-man* is likely to continue to expand to more social groupings and function anew in more diverse interactions. The new uses of *Jaan-e-man* are not incorrect. They are simply new. And, in illustration of the *Diversity Principle*, people are not robotically repeating Bollywood phrases, they are embedding them in highly diverse interactions, creating unique nuances of meaning and functionality.

As Chapters 4 (on YouTube-circulated phrases, dance steps and iconography) and 5 (on YouTube narratives) illustrate, repertoire elements such as ways of talking, gesturing, or moving, and ways of telling a story, circulate swiftly across cyberspace, embedding exponentially in different social contexts and ways of understanding. Ever-morphing YouTube videos illustrate, in time-lapse form, the same processes of re-embedding that went on with "*Jaan-e-man*" in a classroom, over the course of months. Thus, a repertoire approach and the *Diversity Principle* give us a new way of exploring communicative complexity. Rather than linking words and ways of talking to generalized types, we now have the conceptual apparatus to trace those words and other communicative elements back to a history of diverse use and lived experience.

Everyday Metacommentary: An Approach to Analyzing Repertoire

Given the *Diversity Principle* and the ever-multiplying repertoire diversity across individuals, how do people in interaction know which languages, dialects, registers, modalities, media references, or intonation patterns count as relevant? When we define proficiency by a language test and measure it by the individual, it is easy to know what to look at for answers. But when communicating becomes a matter of "repertoire" and relevant knowledge is emergent in interactions, by what mechanisms do we measure the relative efficacy of any interactional move? One important mechanism—the one that we will use to analyze repertoire in this book—is metacommentary.

In any interaction, metacommentary signals an understanding of what a sign means without arbitrarily systematizing communicative elements, but by pointing to that sign's situated communicative value. So, sometimes, people will draw attention to the language being spoken—Spanish, German, or French. At other times, and, I will argue, increasingly in our late-modern era, metacommentary is subtler and the repertoire elements on which it comments are more fine-grained than simple nation-state language categories.

To begin with a not-so-subtle example, let us pay a visit to *Geno's Steaks*. Located on the edge of the Italian Market in South Philadelphia, *Geno's Steaks* generated national media attention in 2006 through metacommentary on language, posting signs around the front windows that said "This is AMERICA: WHEN ORDERING 'SPEAK ENGLISH.'" The metacommentary in this sign makes it explicit that *code*, in the sense of nation-state bounded linguistically distinct code, is the object of attack. Geno's did not specify what *kind* of English should be spoken, or whether the person could have an accent, or what people should wear when they come to his restaurant. They just specified that they want "English."

Everyday metacommentary is often not as explicitly negative as Geno's' sign nor does it always refer to languages. Another common type of metacommentary is on *how* someone speaks. As will be discussed in Chapter 3, "accented speech" often evokes commentary, as when someone asks, after hearing a few unfamiliar pronunciations, "Where are you from?" Or, when non-native speakers are repeatedly asked to repeat themselves, even when they are speaking grammatically well-formed sentences.

But non-native speakers are not the only people whose "accent" draws commentary. Often, varieties of a single language receive metacommentary, and as such, become focal. For example, while Geno's did not specify the *kind* of English people should speak at the restaurant, a news article about the controversy pointed out that "native Philadelphians" speak a certain way, and need to use certain kinds of words to be understood when ordering a cheesesteak, emphasizing that Geno's was not asking that patrons speak "the King's English":

> Of course, it's not as if native Philadelphians speak the King's English either. A Philadelphian might order a cheesesteak by saying something like, "Yo, gimme a cheesesteak wit, will youse?" ("Wit," or "with," means with fried onions.)
>
> *(http://www.foxnews.com/story/0,2933,198757,00. html#ixzz1xDFqjb7b (retrieved 6/8/2012))*

The everyday metacommentary in this news article emphasized that, when ordering at Geno's, more subtle repertoire elements are involved than simply whether "English" or "Spanish" is being spoken. There is also a certain cheesesteak ordering technique in play here that involves a specific pronunciation ("wit" for "with") and even special vocabulary ("Wit" means with fried onions; "Youse" means "you."). So not only languages, but also the way people pronounce them can be objects of everyday metacommentary. And, when people in interaction comment on these features of talk, they raise everyone's awareness of their importance.

One variety of metacomment—the ironic remark—is probably the most widespread form of communicative metacommentary these days. While ironic metacommentary can function as mockery, it can also display many other forms of appreciation for the repertoire range people have at their disposal, and their knowing use of it.

Ben Rampton, for example, has written about how students of German as a foreign language in a London high school ironically use German or "mock German" as he calls it, when they leave that class, to joke around in the school hallways and in other subject classes (transcript adapted from Rampton, 2006):

MOCK GERMAN

Mr. N: as I've said before I get a bit fed up with saying Shshsh
John: LOUDER
Mr. N: you're doing your SATs now
Hanif: VIEL LAUTER SPRECHEN VIEL LAUTER SPRECHEN
          (*translation from German: "speak much louder"*)
Mr. N: (*emphatic*) sshh
John: (*smile voice*) lauter spricken whatever that is

Here, "German" is being used as a language, but to ironically enact a serious and forceful "German" persona, delivering a command directly in opposition to the teacher's "shshsh". Clearly, in this instance, the totality of The German Language as a nation-state bound code is less important than the use of a few German tokens, used here by Hanif to ironically enact a flagrantly unbounded classroom persona.

This type of irony often layers on top of other forms of metacommentary. Just as speaking another language can bring out ironic performances, ways of speaking can also evoke ironic commentary. The news story about Geno's Steaks, for example, brought irony into play by suggesting that probably nobody ordering a cheesesteak in South Philadelphia is speaking "the King's English." Ironic use of address terms is also common: My neighbor calls me a very formal "Dr. Rymes," for example, as she sees me taking out the trash, or my 13-year-old son urges me to "Relax, *homeslice*," when I am trying to rush him out the door to school. These forms of address could be interpreted as mockery, but they are also ways of doing affiliation or sharing hilarity to break up life's inevitable routines.

At times, relentless irony may even seem cynical—perhaps sending a message like, "I've seen it all, and we're all sell-outs. Therefore I take nothing seriously." However, these days, ironic embodiment of a huge range of repertoires has become so common that it can also function to send a message of appreciation and communicative awareness—"I use many ways of speaking and I have witnessed even more. Now I am displaying one of them in a new way because I enjoy how it sounds/looks/feels and the effects it has on other people." Irony, then, rather than being a cynical stance, can be a way of appreciating the vast communicative complexity of contemporary life. Perhaps most accurately, Linda Hutcheon (1994) has described irony as something that "just happens." Rarely do people archly pre-determine the intentions of their ironic comments. Rather, ironic meanings unfold (or fail to!), sometimes unpredictably, based on how much and what types of repertoire overlap, or *comembership* is in play.

The examples given here begin to illustrate the potentially limitless communicative layers that exist in an interaction, and the metacommentary that makes those layers more visible to researchers and more meaningful and relevant to anyone communicating—not simply a pile of experiences that nobody understands.

An individual's "roots" lie not only in some pre-ordained heritage language or culture, but also in the much more random life elements that an individual encounters and absorbs. The meaning of those experiences is often made visible to self and others through metacommentary.

Moreover, metacommentary, like participatory culture, seems to be increasingly prevalent in late modernity. In fact, sites of participatory culture, such as Wikipedia and YouTube, foster the proliferation of metacommentary. Messages on Wikipedia like "this is a stub" metacomment on the type of information in an entry and the need for more. As will be discussed in Chapter 4, videos on YouTube are, primarily, metacommenting on other videos. Often the "original" is no longer identifiable, but lost in a string of video parodies that metacomment on it. In face-to-face interaction as well, metacommentary is rampant. Awareness of ways of speaking and a diversity of communicative routines is also the crux of many comedy acts, YouTube comedians like Kevin Wu, and even feature-length movies such as those of Sasha Baron Cohen.

So, as our communicative repertoires proliferate, so do our means for commenting on them. Through metacommentary, participants give a local order and relevance to the proliferation of communicative means in ways that far surpass simple categories like those evoked in a sign that says "SPEAK ENGLISH."

Review of Chapters in the Book

The next four chapters in this book will each describe elements of communicative repertoire in terms of the method and theory outlined in this first chapter. Chapter 2, *Multilingualisms*, will describe how the term "language" in the traditional sense breaks down when we look more closely at instances of multilingual—or presumably monolingual—talk. Chapters 3 through 5, on *Sounds, Mass Media and Popular Culture*, and *Storytelling*, illustrate how "multilingualism" is just one resource of many that individuals draw on from their communicative repertoire. In a massively multilingual and multicultural world, in which people are often communicating across language difference, often online, communication draws on a wider range of resources.

Chapter 6, *Youthy Repertoires and Adult Repertoires* illustrates how repertoire elements associated with youth and hipness and are not straightforwardly linked to demographic features like "age," or even roles like "teacher" or "student." Given the diverse make-up of classrooms today, youthy repertoires deployed by a teacher in his forties may be lost on a student in her teens.

Chapter 7, *Everyday Encounters with Diversity*, will illustrate how these repertoire elements combine in daily encounters, as individuals discover points of commonality, or misunderstanding, friction, or simply indifference. Here, I illustrate how the performance itself—the artful deployment of one's repertoire and the awareness of repertoire brought to light through metacommentary—brings one individual's communicative repertoire into communion with diverse others.

Finally, Chapter 8, *Communicating Beyond Language*, will bring home the book's central theme—language does not simply map onto other categories like race or culture, but is part of a medley of signifiers that people have available in their repertoires and that are deployed variably across situations. This chapter sums up the implications of a repertoire perspective, providing a new framework for multicultural research and engagement. I will conclude by explaining not only how this approach makes social science sense, by affording more accurate representations of identity and communication, but also, how this approach makes ethical sense by sharpening our perceptions and appreciation of other ways of being human.

2

MULTILINGUALISMS

While giving a workshop to teachers one summer, in a school district facing an exponential increase in Spanish-speaking students, I began by asking the group how many spoke Spanish. Only one of the 30 teachers raised his hand. Then, I asked them all to write down every Spanish word they could think of. After 60 seconds, everyone had at least 20 words on their list. One "non-Spanish-speaking" teacher continued adding to her list during the workshop—just for fun—and at the end of the day, her sheet was covered with hundreds of Spanish words and phrases. These were teachers who initially denied knowing Spanish at all.

Why did the teachers who said they spoke "no Spanish" proceed to write down so many Spanish words? Were they lying to me? Obviously not: They were responding to two different questions, coming from two different perspectives on language. The first question, "Do you speak Spanish?" is asking them about a discrete, bounded, static, defined, nation-state-affiliated code. The second question (or request), "Write down all the Spanish words you know," is asking them to list the Spanish elements of their own communicative repertoire. Asked if they knew Spanish, in a generic sense, they drew a blank; asked to access elements of Spanish in their own active communicative repertoire, they surprised themselves with how much Spanish they knew.

I call the two perspectives in play above the "linguistic monolith" and the "communicative repertoire" approaches to multilingualism. Of these two perspectives on language, the first is clearly the most adhered to in places such as the United States, where until recently any language other than English was taught as a "foreign language." Now we have new descriptive labels, like "world languages" or "heritage languages." This new context calls for a new approach to understanding the role of formerly foreign languages in our lives, and in classrooms. This chapter conceptualizes language as part of one's *communicative repertoire* and illustrates how this new approach has emerged from a context of massive mobility and diversity. Just as new mobility has created participatory cultures and affinity spaces (discussed in Chapter 1) and led us to reconsider what counts as knowledge, it has also made it necessary to rethink what counts as "a language."

In what follows, (and as summarized in Figure 2.1), I will illustrate several ways in which a repertoire perspective on language differs from some of the traditional orthodoxies that conceive of languages as monolithic wholes. Each of these perspectives emerges out of different contexts and engenders different kinds of interactions, valued knowledge, views of language change, and understandings of the role of multilingualism. Then, I will return to the Diversity Principle, explained in Chapter 1, illustrating how, just like other communicative elements (such as clothing, YouTube videos, or tattoo styles), language dynamically takes on many

	The Repertoire Approach	The Linguistic Monolith Approach
Context	Breakdown of geographic constraints via mobility, transnational movement, and internet.	Discrete communities and bounded nation states, limited mobility, centralized control.
Interactional results	Shared spaces (Affinity spaces) and overlap in communicative resources.	Emphasis on distinction and separation of language groups.
Valued knowledge about language	Correctness is less relevant than efficacy, which is contextual and arrived at collaboratively.	Correctness is standardized and arrived at via top-down policing
Role of change and mobility	Languages change over time and increasingly in a context of massive mobility. These multiple "versions" become repertoire elements. Definitions of correctness are arrived at through participatory cultures.	Languages are standardized via top-down processes like dictionaries and grammar books. Language change competes with "correctness."
Role of "mono-" or "multi-" lingualisms	All interactions are multilingual interactions: Monolingualism is a myth (Shohamy, 2007).	Knowing two languages is "double monolingualism" (Heller, 2006; Grosjean, 1985).
Relationship to "The Diversity Principle"	The more widely circulated a language is (like other communicative elements), the more highly diverse the interactions with it will be.	Mobility and new media lead to either the "McDonaldization" of culture and language or the degradation of a "standard."

FIGURE 2.1 Comparison of the Repertoire Approach versus a Linguistic Monolith Approach

different meanings and interactional functions as it spreads to diverse contexts. Applied to multilingualism, a specification of the Diversity Principle is that *the more widely circulated a language is, the more highly diverse the interactions with it will be.*

The Context of a Repertoire Approach to Language

A repertoire approach has the potential to flourish in a context of massive mobility. In such a context, diversity becomes visible, and necessitates new forms of communication across difference. Over the years and around the world there has been variation in how societies react to the presence of multiple languages, ranging from attempted erasure of difference to the embrace of multilingualism. In whatever way they end up addressing language diversity, it is something all societies increasingly face in an age of massive mobility.

Of course "massive mobility" is relative. In 18th-century France, a different language was being spoken roughly every few miles. If an intrepid explorer climbed over a hill to the next village, he might be speaking an unintelligible language. As that adventurous 18th-century climber would discover, mobility also *creates* diversity. In 18th-century France, there was no awareness of linguistic diversity until people began to travel. As long as people stayed in their own village, and they generally did, they experienced homogeneity (Robb, 2007). However, in Gumperz's India (1964, 1965), villagers similarly separated by only a few miles and speaking many different languages, traveled and convened on a common marketplace regularly, where multiple languages had functional value. In that context, language diversity became the norm. And despite the relatively short distances, 1960s' India might have been an example of "massive mobility" in comparison to 18th-century France. Today, our world has become an expanded version of Gumperz's Indian marketplace. As our mobility has increased and communication technologies have bridged continents, the spaces between language groups have become even closer than that climb over the 18th-century hill in France. Simply open up a laptop computer and we can converse with a friend or relative, colleague or business partner on the other side of the planet.

Despite this new global mobility and the experience of diversity it has generated, myriad tentacles of power are always threatening to smother linguistic variation and its contributions to individuals' communicative repertoires. In the 18th century, France was "discovered" when those hundreds of local languages were institutionally erased and a standard French was enforced throughout the nation. And, as Robb writes, "in the land of a thousand tongues, monolingualism became the mark of an educated person" (2007, p. 70). Even today, we live in an era where languages become increasingly standardized and otherwise intelligent people take up public positions that seek to position one language as superior to others. These views also seep into collective perceptions, creating a shared misrecognition: The illusion that there is one language that must be mastered because it is more communicative, more civilized, more patriotic, more practical, more sophisticated, and … just better (Blackledge & Creese, 2010).

There will always be powerful forces that push toward homogenization of an elite (or, actually, middle-class) standard. Evidence of this homogeneous view of language flares up every day and, if unchecked, can exacerbate differences and a sense of "otherness" across groups. For example, the teachers mentioned above, who know many Spanish words—those used by their students and students' families—said they did not speak Spanish. Similarly, these same teachers will say they have students who "do not speak English," despite the obvious wealth of English knowledge these students have and use. Conceptualizing Spanish or English as linguistic monoliths erases the common ground teachers have and could build on with students. On the one hand, almost unconsciously, people—even these teachers in the suburban United States—are becoming communicatively more diverse than ever; on the other hand, the specter of the linguistic monolith keeps that knowledge shrouded.

Today's context has brought about a shift away from linguistic monolith orthodoxies, to an approach that re-envisions languages as one element of a communicative repertoire; researchers in sociolinguistics, applied linguistics and language education are developing new ways to talk about and study the role of language diversity in schools and society. As I will illustrate in the sections that follow, when people operate on the basis of a repertoire perspective on language, they see the role of language change, linguistic knowledge, and multilingualism in new ways—not as threats to a monolithic whole, or their own linguistic expertise, but as potential points of engagement with diversity.

Interactional Results of a Repertoire Perspective on Language

From a repertoire perspective, multilingual classrooms are repositories of languages, free for the sharing. Faced with multiple languages in circulation, parties gravitate toward those languages most suited for communication and shared connection. In contrast to the isolated French villagers in the 1700s, students and teachers in today's linguistically diverse classrooms cannot help but learn about each other's languages. Like the merchants in Gumperz' marketplace who unconsciously used multiple languages when wrangling for bargains or the teachers mentioned above who were surprised by how much Spanish they knew, all members of the multilingual classroom add to their repertoires as they develop ways to communicate across difference.

In contrast, if linguistic monolith assumptions prevail in classrooms of multilingual students, this can foil even the best intentions for positive communication. For example, in conversations with those who teach in multilingual classrooms, certain fears inevitably surface: *If students start using multiple languages in class, won't this create a rift? Won't students think the others are talking about them?* These fears stem from the assumption that languages are unitary wholes and if not understood in their entirety, communication is impossible. The interactional result of this perspective is that people who speak different languages are scared to talk to each other—or they think others are using a different language to talk maliciously about them.

Linguistic monolith assumptions can also lead teachers to believe that if they do not speak the same language as their students or a parent, they cannot communicate *at all*—at least not without expert intermediaries. In communicating with parents, for example, teachers often call on expert intermediaries in the form of "interpreters." This is a common sense approach, and interpreters are often necessary, but, unfortunately, when an interpreter shows up, their presence can invoke the linguistic monolith perspective. Suddenly, the two parties being interpreted are framed as "monolingual." As such, it is assumed that they cannot communicate with each other without the assistance of a third party.

Is it possible that bringing in interpreters actually makes communication worse? Yes. This lack of communication, *brought on* by interpreters, is illustrated in a recent study on parent–teacher conferences (Howard & Lipinoga, 2010). These researchers compared dozens of videotaped parent–teacher conferences—bilingual conferences with an interpreter and monolingual conferences without an interpreter. To their surprise, they found that the non-interpreted meetings were, unanimously, several minutes longer.

Wouldn't a conference take longer when an interpreter had to repeat everything? Wouldn't there be extra time taken for clarification checks? Given these intuitions, one might predict that the interpreted meetings would be at least twice as long. So, why were they so short? It turns out, in these interactions, in most cases, all the not-necessarily-linguistic features that make up a conversation—greetings, eye contact, creating a shared space—failed to occur. These niceties take time and care. But they have little to do with knowing the parents' language. These are also those interactional features that Erickson and Shultz noted as crucial to creating the conditions for comembership, or common ground (see Chapter 1). When an interpreter was present, all communication fell into her hands—in the role of language translator—creating dysfunctional, non-communicative interactions, with little potential for developing comembership or shared affinities between the teacher and parent.

Now, consider how these findings apply to students in a classroom. When students are framed as speaking a "different language," we might disregard other invaluable communicative resources. Instead of drawing on the usual cues—eye contact, gesture, body language—we are left in a communicative vacuum to guess what that person is saying and doing in that other language. With nothing else to go by, this guess might be based on our own fears and insecurities rather than our awareness of the current interaction. Is it really so hard to tell the difference between someone using Spanish to solve a math problem, and using it to talk maliciously about someone else? Most competent speakers of any language can read cues in other languages that hint at what the point of the conversation is. Why not build relationships on the basis of these shared non-linguistic cues? Instead, we often seem to be conditioned by the linguistic monolith perspective to ignore all other aspects of communication.

Both these accounts—of attitudes toward multiple languages in the classroom, and of teachers behaving strangely with interpreters—illustrate interactions that are shrouded by the specter of the linguistic monolith. Participants assume that they are mutually unintelligible to one another because they know little of each other's languages. As such, they abandon the notion that communication is about seeking and finding common ground. Most teachers know a few simple greetings in Spanish: "Hola," or "Buenos Días." Why wouldn't they use those in the parent conferences? If that is too daunting, all teachers know the importance of eye contact and making a newcomer in their classroom feel welcome. Why wouldn't they apply this knowledge to make parents feel welcome? They are worried and intimidated by the "language barrier," an unfortunate metaphor engendered by linguistic monolith orthodoxy.

In contrast, taking a communicative repertoire perspective reveals very different interactional possibilities, producing shared affinity spaces, and overlap in communicative resources. For example, over the last four years, I have observed a Philadelphia area high school English classroom, filled year-to-year with 15–25 students from 10–20 different countries and speaking as many different languages. French, Hindi/Urdu, Punjabi, Spanish, Haitian Creole or Liberian English can be heard across the room on any given day. The teacher, "Mr. Z," born and raised in Philadelphia, speaks very little of any of these languages, but he never, unlike other teachers in the same school, commands that the students speak "English Only." Nevertheless, I have never witnessed an incident in which students think they are talking behind each other's backs, or Mr. Z worries they are talking maliciously about him.

Instead, there seems to develop among the students a desire to know each other's languages and to try them out. French-speakers from Burkina Faso and Guinea, for example, periodically use their French during English class, often to metacommentaries of envy from the other multilingual (but non-French speaking) students, as below:

OH, FRENCH!
((*The students are watching a movie and the initial credits rolling are written in French*))

Aiche: Oh, French! ((*sounding pleasantly surprised*))
Krysta: Oh, yeah—you can read it.
Virginia: I'm jealous!

In the year this interaction was recorded there were several students from French-speaking countries in the class and French seemed to emerge as the language other students wished they knew. The previous year, Hindi/Urdu seemed to be the language of interest, and the year before that, when there were several Spanish speakers in the class, Spanish was the desirable language. While these students were in an English-medium class, reading and discussing English literature, they developed a desire to know each other's non-English languages.

This desire grew in a context in which Mr. Z respected the other languages—he did not feel students were talking about each other. Nor did he believe their use of other languages was detracting from his teaching. Indeed, it seemed that students' language use fostered community in his room. He did not treat the presence of other languages as monolithic threats to his teaching, his connection with students, or their ability to build positive relationships with each other. In contrast, it fostered community.

This classroom context, filled with multiple languages, also illustrates how a classroom can be a space for participatory culture. As students learned elements of a traditional English curriculum—reading novels and poetry, writing and discussing literature in English—they also learned about each other, their languages, and their countries of origin. Like the self-motivated, interested engines that drive participatory culture, these students had incentive to be there, because they were an instrumental part of the knowledge production of that class. Because their languages were valued and not silenced, because they could talk to each other and witness as others valued their contributions, they grew as a community that could engage in real discussions. As Seniors in high school, already heading toward graduation, and many with jobs to do, siblings or babies of their own to take care of, they had little incentive to show up for class each day. And yet, with one or two exceptions they did.

A recent classroom project illustrates the participatory culture that developed there. In their final semester, this class produced a book of student memoirs, *Our Stories* (see Figure 2.2), all written in English. These ranged from stories of a bucolic Liberian childhood full of soccer and mangos, to a daughter refusing an arranged

FIGURE 2.2 Participatory Culture in a High School Classroom: A Collection of Student Memoirs

marriage and being ostracized from the family, to a girl giving birth to her own son, despite being rejected by her family for making that choice (see Figure 2.3 below). Each student read the book voraciously and they commented on each other's stories spontaneously in class and during an in-class "coffee house" reading held by the teacher. Before the reading, I visited the room after the book had been out for a few days, and the students were still carrying it around, pulling it out to read in idle moments. As class ended, a large Haitian boy called out to a tiny girl from Mexico, "Hey, I really liked your story. It made me cry. I'm serious."

While this book was written in English, its production and substance—the stories were several pages each—emerged from an interactional context where students valued each other's repertoires. Mr. Z never silenced the presence of different languages in this room and in this way he helped turn the classroom into a

	Type of Interaction	Examples	Descriptive Research and Associated Term(s)
More monolithic	Bilinguals who keep their languages completely separate. No mixing.	French ONLY in francophone classrooms (Heller, 2006); "Caught between Languages" (Mori, 1999)	*Double Monolingualism* (Grosjean, 1995; Heller, 2006)
	Bilinguals who switch languages freely as communicatively necessary.	A Day in the Life of Alex	*Flexible Bilingualism* (Creese and Blackledge, 2010; 2011) *Translanguaging* (García, 2009) *Dynamic Lingualism* (Flores, 2012) *Poly-lingualism* (Jørgensen, 2010)
	People who know a few words of another language and use them in select contexts.	London Youth: Punjabi speakers for Bhangra fanship. Mr. Z's class: "Hand me a computer, Jaan- e-maan"	*Crossing* (Rampton, 1995); *Truncated Language Use* (Blommaert, 2008)
More repertoire-like	People (ALL people) who use combinations of languages and ways of speaking when they communicate.	London Adults negotiating phone calls. John Ashbury poetry. A Rose in Spanish Harlem	*Contemporary Urban Vernaculars* (Rampton, 2010) *Heteroglosia* (Bakhtin, 1985)

FIGURE 2.3 Types of Multilingual Interactions

space where students also shared about their lives. The participatory culture that developed emerged in large part from the respect this teacher nurtured for the range of communicative repertoires in the classroom.

To summarize, interactions between speakers of different languages can change dramatically once speakers free themselves from the assumptions of the linguistic monolith. Those teachers who fear that students speaking other languages are insulting the others and using language to create divisions might be right, but only if they check all their other communicative resources at the door and uphold a monolithic standard for how languages function in that classroom. Similarly, those who believe that the interpreter is the sole conduit for communication in parent–teacher conferences across languages might be right, but only if that teacher forgets all the other features of her communicative repertoire—greetings, eye-gaze, welcoming posture and tone, checking to be sure you are understood—and lets the interpreter be the sole vehicle for communication. The linguistic monolith perspective can be self-perpetuating.

Once teachers and students are permitted to view their languages as part of a broader communicative repertoire and as a way to learn about each other, many new kinds of interactions are possible and new knowledge begins to be recognized and relevant. Rather than relying entirely on outside language experts, people begin to share what resources they have with each other.

Role of Standardized Linguistic Knowledge in a Repertoire Perspective on Language

The varied resources of individuals, however, are often put down in favor of a single standard. Just as the many languages circulating in France in the 1700s were dismissed by French-speakers as invariably quaint set-pieces or simply barbarous and sub-human (the word for one of those languages, "Basque," also meant "cow"), the multiple languages and ways of speaking circulating in the United States today have faced many detractors. Many states, attempting to keep this language diversity at bay, have created laws declaring English their official language, or banishing bilingual education. Politicians often promote these policies on the basis that English (or French, or ...) are monolithic wholes and the unity of our democratic nation will crumble in the face of other languages.

Once we get away from the assumption that knowing and using additional languages detracts from our unity and communicative facility, and instead view languages as adding to one's communicative repertoire, creating the potential for common ground, then zeroing in on one standard is not necessary—not to promote unity, and certainly not to promote positive interactions and learning in a classroom. Still, even today, teachers' choices are influenced by the specter of the monolithic standard. Just as teachers may worry that students who speak other languages are talking about them or each other, they may also fear that other languages in their classrooms prevent students from acquiring content knowledge—especially if the content is The English Language. Under a linguistic monolith perspective, the presence of other languages prevents the learning of English; from a repertoire perspective, other languages are an enriching component of the English classroom.

To exemplify, let us take another look at Mr. Z's classroom, where, over the last four years, there have been several students from Liberia: Speakers of "Liberian English." For these students, the specter of a monolithic standard looms large. In conversations with myself and other researchers, these students have talked about how they did not feel their Liberian English was "real" English. They felt, as Liberian speakers placed in an English class for "English language learners," they had no language at all. Many of them wished they spoke another language (other than English) in the classroom. The logic was that if they knew a language such as "French" or "Spanish" or "Hindi/Urdu," they would have one "real" language they already knew, since they were in a class of kids learning English.

These students seem to have internalized a perspective on English as only one standard, a perspective that reduces their form of English to Not English. And, in the face of the other world languages circulating in the room, Liberian English was demoted to not-language. Rather than recognizing Liberian English as a language that had been fully functional for them, one that they had been born and raised in, and continued to use among themselves and with their families, the institutional imposition of the category of "English Language Learner" labeled it as not English or, as many of the Liberian students came to refer to their own way of speaking, "broken English."

Fortunately, these students came to an English class in which English is not treated as a linguistic monolith and nor are the diverse languages of the students. In fact, motivated by the several Liberian English speakers in the class over the years, the teacher, Mr. Z, had studied the country's history and its language and he had read memoirs written about life in the country (as well as other countries represented in his classroom). He also encouraged the students to share. Sometimes the Liberian English speakers in the class, with their teacher's encouragement, would take those few moments of free-time before the bell rang to explain a few things about their own language, explicitly naming it "Liberian English." Once, in more official classroom time, after reading the words "Thiefy" and "Rogue" (for burglar) in a novel by the Liberian author, Helene Cooper, a Liberian student, Janetta, now the expert, explained, "People call out 'thiefy'. That's a Liberian English word." Here, Janetta did not translate "thiefy" as if she were a human dictionary ("Thiefy means *burglar*"). Instead, she provided an example of it in use—"people call out ...,'" imbuing it with her own personal experience and, perhaps, enjoying the connection of her life to the lives depicted in the published memoir they were reading.

By bringing examples like this into the classroom, this teacher illustrates a perspective on knowledge and on what counts as language by building a shared repertoire with his students. This repertoire includes words like "thiefy," but also a habit for engaging intellectually. Students come to understand that their words are a valid part of a larger conversation as they share—and contest—knowledge. There are also plenty of students in the class who would, if they did not agree with Janetta, contest the definition of "thiefy" or even the validity of Janetta's knowledge. But this contesting would not be top-down and arbitrary ("That is not proper English!"), it would be critical and participatory ("I never heard people say that in Liberia!"), just as people build, debunk, and take down entries from Wikipedia.

I have observed other ELL classrooms full of students with similar multilingual backgrounds to those in Mr. Z's classroom, but taught more traditionally. In one such class, the students were silent and at the edge of sleep for the entire session as a teacher reiterated rules about conjunctions and took them through practice exercises. This was a grim instantiation of the linguistic monolith orthodoxy—the practice of, piece-by-piece, teaching linguistic knowledge as if it were immutable and presuming that, once it is mastered on a worksheet, it will be useful. This type of class will be most successful at driving multilingual students away from school, where they will learn English just fine (Tse, 2001), but will miss out on the benefits of participatory cultures of school of the kind that developed in Mr. Z's class.

So, what is the role of standardized linguistic knowledge in a repertoire perspective? Like other elements of communication, linguistic knowledge is a repertoire component. However, linguistic knowledge cannot stand alone as a monolithic portrait of what it means to communicate. From a repertoire perspective, there is no standard but that which is arrived at in communication. "Thiefy" was correct and relevant in the English classroom when Janetta was explaining how it is used in Liberia. It was correct and relevant in Helene Cooper's memoir—even if one could imagine a naive copy-editor trying to change it. The highest standard for language is one that includes multiple repertoires and recognizes how they function. Mr. Z's classroom flourishes as a context for learning English by becoming a participatory culture in which students expand their repertoires in multiple ways, just one of which is the acquisition of "academic English."

Role of Change and Mobility

It is highly possible that nobody shouts out "thiefy" in Liberia anymore. When I brought up the word with a graduate student who has traveled there recently, she said she had never heard it. What happened? Were the memoirist (also a *New York Times* reporter) and the Philadelphia area high school student both wrong? And, if so, why were they both wrong in the same way? While Helene Cooper's memoir was published in 2008, her family fled Liberia as it broke out into civil war in the 1980s. The Liberia she writes about is not the Liberia of today. Janetta's family fled Liberia, in the early 2000s as refugees from a war-torn country. Over 30—or even 10—years, it is likely that life and language have changed there. In the United States, which has been relatively stable in comparison, using words from the 1980s (groovy!) or even the early 2000s (fierce!) can date you. It might be that using "thiefy" dates you in Liberia.

Whatever the case, the possibilities raised by the word "thiefy" illustrate the interplay of two crucial elements: language change and mobility. Whether people say "thiefy" in Liberia anymore or not, it is undeniable that languages change over time. The evidence is all around us. We do not use English the way people did in Shakespeare's time. Our kids do not use English like we do. These are obvious statements. Obvious, but incompatible with a linguistic monolith lens, in which language is conceived as something unitary and unchanging to be learned and then used immutably. New media and mobility make it foolish for anyone to labor under this illusion. Not only do languages change, they change differently in different places. This poses a problem for someone who wants to pin a language down as a singular monolith, which taken to its logical extreme would have language change leading us down a slippery slope to unintelligibility. Not so for someone who takes a repertoire perspective. Seen this way, the dynamism of language adds to the richness of individuals' repertoires, and it fosters and flourishes in participatory culture.

The "thiefy" example illustrates how change becomes even more interesting in a context of massive mobility. Helene Cooper and Janetta are both people who were born in Liberia and live in the United States now. They both have a memory of the word "thiefy" and how it is used in "Liberia." I put that in quotes, because now they are creating a Liberia of their shared memories, one that is real to them, but might no longer exist in the geographical space called Liberia. Multiply this by all the Liberian English that transnational Liberians have brought with them to the United States, and you can see that the "Liberian English" of those in the USA may become very different from the Liberian English spoken by those who remain in Liberia. Some elements, like the word "thiefy" may be stuck in the U.S. version. But this does not mean the U.S. version is frozen. Other words probably enter into the U.S. version, or leave it, but remain in the Liberian version. So, mobility leads to many more possibilities for what "Liberian English" might be. The language will inevitably change over time, but add mobility to the mix, and it is changing in different ways in different places. These changes are clearly based on what speakers need language for; living in Philadelphia rather than Liberia inevitably places different communicative demands on speakers.

If one were to take Liberian English *in Liberia* as a "standard," now, not only is Liberian English in the USA not "English," it is not even "Liberian English." From a repertoire perspective, Liberian English is part of an entire communicative repertoire and words such as "thiefy," when called on to build common ground and share knowledge are functional parts of that repertoire, whether or not they are still used in "*Liberian* Liberian English." So language change and mobility pose a double threat to a monolithic notion of standard language. In the face of language change and mobility, we need to flex our communicative repertoire.

This repertoire flexibility becomes even more important once we consider not only that people are physically mobile, but also that people are virtually mobile, using the internet and new media to make connections across the usual borders. Many multilingual students in the U.S. maintain relationships with family via Skype or cell phone, or, slightly less directly, via other kinds of social media.

New media have also distributed our sources of authority—making them participatory. As we converse across borders and need information about languages, our sources also span the globe. Dictionaries may have at one time been a standardizing force, authorizing meanings of words at least until publication of the next edition. However, dictionaries are no longer only created through top-down editorial processes. Now, dictionaries—at least the ones most people use—are participatory. People now find "definitions" on Google, Urban Dictionary, or Websters online. And, in addition to dictionaries, people can easily call on their social networks via Facebook or other internet-based infrastructures, to find answers to language questions (or any others).

Moreover, the results can be more communicatively fine-grained. Just as Janetta explained, "people call out, 'thiefy'," giving a living example of how the word might work in an interaction, Googling a definition can lead not only to dictionary entries, but also to entire blog strands about ways people use that word. If I ask Google, "How to say 'happy birthday' in Brazil," I get an answer like this, "Parabéns—which actually means congratulations. You can also say 'Feliz Aniversario' which means literally 'happy anniversary', but parabéns is by far the most common." I could take this at face value (it was ranked by other readers as the best answer), or I could read through the blog and see what others have to say. What counts as "happy birthday" in Brazilian Portuguese is a participatory agreement. But that agreement is not set in stone. Someday, people might start saying "Feliz Aniversario" more often on birthdays. And we can know immediately if it seems right. Not by asking an authority or consulting a language textbook, but by checking Google.

Calling on participatory culture is a way of checking the validity of one's repertoire. It is like asking a friend or a colleague rather than looking something up in the dictionary, a grammar book, or a textbook. In the face of rapid change and massive linguistic diversity, participatory culture is the most communicatively viable source of information. Just as someone online could check a meaning of a word through their Facebook network, Wikipedia, or dictionary.com, a student in Mr. Z's English class can check the viability of his repertoire by engaging with students in that classroom's participatory culture.

Role of Multilingualism

From the monolith perspective, languages exist as discrete, compartmentalized and, at times, daunting wholes. From the repertoire perspective, combining languages in a single interaction happens effortlessly every day. As I will illustrate below, *every interaction is a "multilingual" interaction.* On our way to that final point, let us trace through the different possibilities for how languages can combine in "multilingual interaction," from the most monolithic possibilities, to the more flexible and repertoire-oriented instances (outlined in Figure 2.3).

Given the increasing language change and mobility discussed so far, and all the potential liberty and linguistic richness that comes with it, the belief in "one standard French" or "one standard Hindi/Urdu" is impossible to maintain. Nevertheless, there are some orthodoxies that tell us languages exist this way and that to speak two languages means to speak both "perfectly" and *separately*. This means even many bilinguals (perhaps especially teachers) treat speaking another language, not as a chance to draw on some of their repertoire, but as a display of another form of expertise.

Monica Heller (2006, building on Grosjean, 1985) has called this need for purity and separation of bilingual competence, "double monolingualism," illuminating the awkward interactional knots that result when insisting on linguistic purity in a bilingual community or classroom. Writing about a francophone school in Toronto, she shows that when various activities (discussing a flyer, written in English) or subject matter (upper level science) call for the use of at least some words and phrases in English, rather than use these English words or phrases, teachers develop elaborate strategies to awkwardly speak only French; this, despite the fact that they are bilingual individuals living in a bilingual community. In the following excerpt, for example, a teacher was simultaneously translating into French a flyer, written in English, about all the career opportunities available for those who major in the natural sciences. As she translated, she hesitated and allowed a student to read the word "forensic" aloud for her. Oddly, though the English word was written on the paper in front of her, she repeated the English word only after a student, Marcel, supplied it (transcript adapted from Heller, 2006, p. 90):

French flyer being simultaneously translated by Aline, the teacher	English translation
Aline:	
Tu peux devenir ingénieur chimique	You can become a chemical engineer
Tu peux devenir euh vendeur de produits chimiques	You can become uh a salesperson for chemical products
Tu peux travailler pour Hydro-Ontario	You can work for Hydro-Ontario
Tu peux travailler comme les policiers comme chimiste euh	You can work like the police as a chemist uh
Marcel:	
forensic	*forensic*
Aline:	
Forensic ouais	*forensic* yeah
Tu peux enseigner	You can teach

Aline, here, accepts the word "forensic" supplied by a student, rather than simply reading the word off the page, almost as if she is unable to access her own English proficient side. In a francophone school, and under the cloud of linguistic monolith orthodoxies, she resists using any of her English language to communicate. As a result, she becomes awkward with both languages.

This pedagogical conundrum echoes the dilemma Kyoko Mori describes when she writes of her "Japanese" language and "English" language as two different entities to be kept separate. In her memoir, *Polite Lies* (1997), Mori struggles with these homogeneous portraits of language. She was born in Japan but raised in the United States, and describes herself as "caught between languages." Her infrequent trips back to Japan fill her with anxiety as she vacillates between English and Japanese, the "two stations" of her mind:

> I cannot shed my fear of the Japanese language. When the plane begins its descent toward Tokyo or Osaka and the final sets of announcements are made in the two languages, I do not try to switch from the English station of my mind to the Japanese. I turn the dial a little closer to the Japanese station without turning off the English, even though my mind will fill with static and the Japanese I speak will be awkward and inarticulate. I am willing to compromise my proficiency in Japanese so that I can continue to think the thoughts I have come to value in English.
>
> *(p. 19)*

Here, Mori speaks of the difficulty of switching "the dial" completely to one language or another. Her use of radio stations as a metaphor for her two languages illuminates her resistance, yet underlying acquiescence to the double monolingualism perspective. Just as radio stations fill with static when not accurately tuned in, Mori's Japanese becomes "awkward and inarticulate" if the Japanese station is not fully compartmentalized. Yet, she fears, if she does tune it all the way, her English "station" will be completely gone; as she goes back to speaking pure Japanese, her English thoughts will vanish. Mori's English and Japanese proficiencies are set, like push buttons on a car radio. For Mori, Japanese is something she takes a plane to go to, and the presence of English at all in such a context seems only to create static. Conceptualizing her repertoire as two set radio stations—or two pristine linguistic monoliths, or, to use Heller's phrase, two monolingualisms—keeps Mori from flexing her repertoire to accommodate to the communicative needs of multiple settings. As such, she sees herself as "caught" between languages.

Imagine, in contrast to either the linguistic purity of the francophone school day, or the annual trip to Japan, a day in the life of an immigrant boy, Alex, who lives in a suburban edge city near Philadelphia. Born in Acapulco, Mexico, he came here as a sixth-grader. As a seventh-grader, from morning to evening, his day included the typical activities of a 13-year-old in the United States: He ate breakfast, walked to school, went to classes, walked home and chatted with friends, helped his mother make dinner, helped his brother with homework. However, in each of these activities, the role of Spanish and English would change.

Unlike Mori who would fly, perhaps once a year, to Japan, and would feel a momentous struggle "between languages" as she did so, Alex shifts between languages virtually from activity to activity. He chats in Spanish on the way to school, becomes silent in technology class, socializes in English in his ELL class, and uses Spanish to explain problems to a friend in an otherwise English-speaking math class. On the way home, he uses Spanish with his friends and to call out greetings to adults. Once home, he uses Spanish with his mother as they make dinner, but effortlessly moves in and out of English with his little brother, who has had all his schooling in the United States, as he helps him with his homework.

Alex speaks two languages, English and Spanish, but he is not a double monolingual. As one moves with him throughout his day, it is clear he is not making the kinds of struggles that Mori, the memoirist, reflects on and that Aline, the francophone teacher, enacts. Instead, Alex draws on each language as part of his individual repertoire, selecting the elements of each that he needs to accomplish a math problem, help his mother, socialize in English class, or do homework with his brother.

So far, I have described cases in which people who speak more than one language, seem to "switch" in and out of languages: Mori, the memoirist, and Aline, the teacher, resist such switching and attempt to keep their codes distinct; Alex switches languages from activity to activity, and sometimes even midsentence. But these days, multilingual interactions are often not characterized by such clear-cut switching. Instead, a speaker needs only a word or two in a language or two to have a multilingual interaction. A student who says "Hand me a computer, Jaan-e-man" in Mr. Z's class is not really "code-switching" in the same way. A teacher who welcomes a parent into her classroom with "Hola," one of the few Spanish words in her repertoire, is not code-switching. And yet, this form of multilingualism has the potential to build common ground between speakers of multiple languages as each participant expands their repertoire.

To summarize, some individuals who speak two languages, limit the contact between those languages, functioning as "double monolinguals." Others, as the day in the life of Alex illustrates, use those two languages as part of one larger communicative repertoire, and the need to block off the two (or more) languages from each other vanishes. Others, who, unlike Aline or Alex, do not have "full" command of an additional language, use whatever they do have in interactions with multilingual others. There is no wall between languages, as in two monolingualisms; the languages in play need not be fully formed as something one could switch into, the way one pushes a button for another radio station. There is no need to know an entire language (impossible anyway) to partake in multilingual interactions. This is one way we are all multilingual, and have at least some minimal ability to call on words we know from other languages.

What about those who truly do not know any words in any other language? Aren't they monolingual? No. If there are such people, who perhaps grew up in a remote English-speaking outpost with no contact with mass media and who, as a result, really do not know any other "languages" labeled as such, they will have many different ways of speaking to different people and in various settings. It is unlikely that a mother in that remote outpost will speak the same way to her four-year-old daughter as she will to her spouse. Her 12-year-old son will probably develop some unique ways of speaking with his friends. And he will probably speak to his grandmother in very different ways. People will also have different ways of speaking over lunch with friends, in a business meeting, or during a romantic dinner. It would be impossible to live a full life—even a basic, boring life—without developing these various ways of addressing people, forming connections with them, and participating in life's routines. So, in that sense, nobody—even those who literally know no words from any language other than their mother tongue—is "monolingual."

As non-monolinguals, we are always engaging in multilingual interactions. Not only do we change languages and ways of speaking from activity to activity, we use bits and pieces of languages and ways of speaking to shift the way we talk within a single conversation or within even a single sentence. It is not awkward at all to use multiple languages and ways of speaking this way. Imagine, for example, someone saying this during an increasingly unruly class discussion: "Excuse me sir, you're outta line!" While the first half of the sentence is uttered in a polite, formal tone, the second half is a more informal, idiomatic way of speaking. This type of combination, we can call it "rapid-fire formal/informal" or "Frankly my dear, I don't give a damn" style, has the potential to produce dramatic effects. This way of speaking communicates a layered message quickly, precisely through the combination of ways of speaking.

Rapid-fire switches happen all the time, not only between "formal" and "informal" but also between many other activity-specific ways of speaking—and between multiple languages. "Formal" and "informal" ways of speaking are not locked into those activity contexts. You do not have to be at a formal dinner to use "formal" language. You do not have to be in the sandbox to use "informal" language. These, and many other ways of speaking combine fruitfully all the time. Similarly, languages combine to yield similar communicative effects (e.g., "Hand me the computer, Jaan-e-man") precisely through the contrast in languages. And, a speaker does not have to be in French class to speak French or in English class to speak English. Both might happen and work well together. And, these "mixed" ways of speaking are often neither self-conscious nor exotic; these combinations can happen as un-self-consciously as any other way of speaking.

Combining languages and ways of speaking is not aberrant behavior. This is an essential component of all communication. And yet, while researchers in applied linguistics, sociolinguistics, and language education agree these combining tendencies are an important contemporary communicative reality, they seem to be facing a crisis in how to describe this phenomenon. Older terms, such as "code-switching," seem to reify the linguistic monolith, suggesting, as Mori does in her reflections, that speakers switch between language "codes" in complete ways, like pressing buttons for your favorite stations on the car radio.

Lately, new descriptive terms, listed below, have proliferated in an effort to more accurately describe multilingual interactions of the kind I have discussed above (see also Figure 2.3):

> Flexible bilingualism (Creese and Blackledge, 2011)
> Translanguaging (García, 2009)
> Dynamic Lingualism (Flores, 2012)
> Poly-lingualism (Jørgensen 2008)
> Crossing (Rampton, 1995)
> Truncated language use (Blommaert, 2008)
> Contemporary urban vernaculars (Rampton, 2010)

Each of these terms has arisen out of research in different interactional contexts, and focuses on slight variations in how language is working, each adding another component to how languages are being used as part of a repertoire speakers draw on flexibly and strategically. The first four terms, *flexible bilingualism*, *translanguaging*, *dynamic lingualism* and *polylingualism*, describe situations where bilingual individuals, like Alex, the bilingual boy mentioned above, draw on their languages selectively for different activities and when talking with different types of people.

The next two terms, *crossing* and *truncated language use*, attend to slightly different types of multilingual interactions—those in which one party clearly has a more minimal set of linguistic resources at hand. In *Crossing* (1995), Rampton describes how, like those kids who call out "Jann-e-mann" in Mr. Z's class, kids in a London high school use South Asian words and ways of speaking to connect with their classmates and engage in Bhangra music fanship with them, *crossing* into another language to make social connections with another language group. Blommaert uses the term *truncated language use* to contrast this kind of language facility with the more solidly bilingual type described by the first four terms (and illustrated above in the cases of Aline, Mori, and Alex). By using the word "truncated," Blommaert emphasizes the limited extent of the additional language being called on. An English teacher who, knowing only a few words of Spanish, surprises herself by calling out "hola!" to her students, might be an example of someone who has what Blommaert calls a *truncated* repertoire.

Finally, Rampton uses the term *contemporary urban vernaculars* (2010) to describe the third kind of more inclusive language flexibility I have also attempted to describe above: By using this term, he describes not only the use of multiple ways of speaking, but also the way multiple "languages" blend to form urban vernaculars that are polylingual and polydialectal. He illustrates how, like the students in Mr. Z's class, adults in London blend repertoire elements like Punjabi words, Jamaican creole, and traditional London vernacular freely in conversation. For

Rampton, this is not a "truncated" form of language use, but a fully functional way everyday people draw on their communicative repertoire.

These terms have begun to usefully label some types of multilingual communication and to capture how languages work in concert with each other as elements of an individual's inevitably multilingual communicative repertoire. As Creese and Blackledge have pointed out (2011), these "complex linguistic repertoires bear the traces of past times and present times, of lives lived locally and globally" (p. 1206). Given this complexity, they also suggest that Bakhtin (1981) may have come up with the most adequate term for contemporary multilingual communication: Heteroglossia.

Bakhtin was not a sociolinguist, but a philosopher and literary critic, and "heteroglossia," is only minimally about the combining of languages, in the traditional sense of nation-state-bounded codes such as Spanish or French. Rather, Bakhtin introduced the concept of heteroglossia as a way of capturing the baroque complexity of interaction between people (or, rather, characters in novels) on different biographical trajectories.

Literary and artful perspectives on language instantly open up a world of repertoire diversity, and the pleasure of expression it affords. Even a classic pop song can illustrate the pleasure of slight shifts in repertoire of the "Frankly my dear, I don't give a damn" style, as in Ben E. King's *Spanish Harlem*, when the direct "I lose control" is swiftly followed by "I have to beg your pardon!":

> There is a rose in Spanish Harlem
> A red rose up in Spanish Harlem
> With eyes as black as coal that look down in my soul
> And start a fire there and then I lose control
> I have to beg your pardon

The subtlety of this shift illustrates something more delicate than simply a change in "register" from one monolithic "informal" register to another monolithic "formal" one. Instead the pleasure comes from the subtlety of their co-occurrence and their more subtle distinctions from one another. The creative juxtaposition of repertoire elements—whether we label it "heteroglossia" or "frankly my dear, I don't give a damn" style—marks sentimental songs such as "Spanish Harlem" as well as more elite forms of literary genius, like the poetry of John Ashbery. Ashbery regularly makes readers flinch with the joys of language by abruptly calling on a huge repertoire range, as here, in the poem *The Short Answer*, where he juxtaposes "rascal," "pince-nez," the stock query, "did you ever hear from …?" the often meaningless, "particularly" and other semi-fossilized phrases (Ashbery, 2012):

> …
> The rascal jumped over the fence.
> I'm wiping my pince-nez now. Did you ever hear from

The one who said he'd be back once it was over,
Who eluded me even in my sleep?
That was a particularly
Promising time we thought.

The poetry of John Ashbery often calls on this type of mixture: The silly pomposity of wiping one's "pince-nez" immediately after "the rascal jumped over the fence"; the wry impossibility that this must be a "particularly promising time." These Ashberian combinations yield an oddly ironic effect, evoking the pleasure of living through language, but also the strange juxtaposition of importance and triviality. "Mixing languages"—in "double monolingualism" sense that "pince-nez" might be considered a "French" word amid English words—is not what brings this poetry its charm—the entire stanza is a carnival of different ways of using language, or, as Bakhtin would call it, heteroglossia.

This literary version of heteroglossia is consistent with the repertoire perspective: Each person or novelistic character or poetic evocation is drawing on a different individual repertoire of languages, ways of speaking and other communicative elements. In this respect, whether we are looking at a transnational classroom, an encounter with a popular song, or the reading of a poem, *every interaction is a "multilingual" interaction*.

Relationship to the Diversity Principle

After all this discussion of language change, mobility and new media, the participatory nature of new language "standards," and the recognition that every interaction is "multilingual," it is odd to recall another belief, engendered in part by linguistic monolith orthodoxies: The belief that these forces will lead to homogenization of language. Just as some fear that globalization leads to "McDonaldization" of culture, some also see globalization as a threat to linguistic diversity. Isn't everyone learning English now? Doesn't everyone pick up the same phrases and styles that they see on TV? Aren't people around the globe wearing the same New York Yankees caps they have all seen on the same YouTube videos? All these observations might have elements of truth to them. However, they miss one crucial point:

> The Diversity Principle: *The more widely circulated a communicative element is, the more highly diverse the interactions with it will be.*

Setting aside all the other elements of communication that are included in this principle—sounds, routines, gestures, clothing, accessories (to be discussed in the coming chapters)—a specification of the Diversity Principle, applied to the role of multilingualism is as follows:

The more widely circulated a language *is, the more highly diverse the interactions with it will be.*

From this perspective, let us take English as a case example. Acknowledging that English is spoken increasingly around the globe does not entail a threat to language diversity. To the contrary, just as a Yankees cap means very different things when worn at a Philly's game, a Yankees game, a Jay-Z concert, a nightclub in Burkina Faso, or a street protest in Egypt, "English" takes up very different roles in individuals' repertoires as it disperses across the globe and through the internet. Some common examples of widely used English in India illustrate this point: The Hindi-influenced, "What is your good name?" will be used in India rather than "What is your full name"; "Today morning" and "Yesterday night" may be used in place of "This morning," or "Last night" (Baldridge, 2002).

Inevitably, some people will put these varieties of English in hierarchical order, claiming that some are superior to others. Or, in India, they might insist that variations originate in the "original" British colonial language. Some speakers of Global Englishes like to keep English pure—separate, as its own monolingualisms—in order to preserve the fantasy of some magic, English-centered, bourgeois edge. Others may have allegiances to the kinds of English that are imbued with local languages, grammatical constructions, and routines. In any case, from a repertoire perspective, all these Englishes are potential elements of an individual's expanding repertoire. Just as there is huge variation in how or where one should wear a Yankees cap—people are using it for any number of functions or identity displays—there is huge functional and expressive variation in how people use English internationally.

Regardless of people's varied beliefs about what English should be and what it can do for them, in practice, in international settings, it is likely that the "native" speakers of English will be the ones who need to accommodate to whatever variety of English is spoken in the context they are visiting. In his updated brief on the English language (*English Next*, 2006), Graddol reports that international business people often hold their meetings in English, but find them to be more productive when *no* "native speakers" of English are present. The desirability and functionality of a mythical native speaker standard seems to have completely vanished in such contexts.

So, as English has permeated more and more contexts, it has not decimated the local character of those contexts, as a monolithic colonial invader. Instead, as English enters new settings and is used by different people with different repertoires to accomplish diverse tasks, in each new milieu, it takes on a character of its own. And, while local languages can be threatened by this incursion, English also provides a medium for the conveyance of local identity. As people begin to speak English more and more as a local language, "speakers will signal their nationality, and other aspects of their identity" (Graddol, 2006, p. 114) through English. So, indeed, as Graddol's report on the state of global English makes clear, an even more fine-grained specification of the diversity principal may be as follows:

> *The more widely circulated* English *is, the more highly diverse the interactions with it will be.*

Moreover, paradoxically, the more widely circulated English is, the more important it becomes that individuals learn other languages, including other Englishes. In many contexts, English has become a necessary, but not sufficient means for communicating.

In Closing

People today are growing up and into a very different communicative context than they were a generation ago. Communicative needs have changed. We cannot pretend that giving a student a frozen, standardized version of another language in addition to their mother tongue will prepare them adequately to be a full participant in the contemporary world. Indeed, the opposite may be the case. As Graddol remarks at the end of his last report on the English language:

> Immigrants to English-speaking countries may need to learn the language of their host society, but increasingly, that may be insufficient. Since they tend to live and work alongside other ethnic communities, they may find they have to learn other languages as well.
>
> *(2006, p. 118)*

The examples throughout this chapter have illustrated that both these immigrants, and their teachers, will be incorporating languages other than English into their repertoires. This new multilingualism emerges out of real communicative needs brought on by mobility and new media. People's communicative repertoires are expanding by necessity. But this growing embrace of multiple languages may also provide us with a means of finding connection across difference and developing more participatory sources of knowledge and validation. My examples have centered on how youth use multilingualism in even minimal ways to connect to one another, and how teachers, once their fear of being judged for "correctness" is ameliorated, can also use language to begin to connect to multilingual students and their families and to develop participatory cultures in their classrooms. Further, what once was considered one "language" contains multiple languages and endless possibilities for creative expression. Once the specter of the linguistic monolith is removed, and we focus on developing repertoires for engagement, multiple languages become a resource to be nurtured not feared, and a necessary resource for any individual to fully partake in their world.

3

YOU HAD ME AT "HELLO"

Sounds as Repertoire

Imagine all the sounds of languages you might hear while sitting in the food court at the international terminal of a busy U.S. airport. Whether you are in New York or Atlanta, Chicago or Los Angeles, probably many of the voices on the Public Address system, will sound nearly identical: "Maintain control of your bags at all times ... To ensure flights leave on time, arrive at your gate 30 minutes prior to departure ... ." The Spanish-language versions of these announcements also will hardly change from airport to airport. But, then, a new voice awkwardly announces the name of some individuals: "Maria Vill-la and Jo-a-quin Parade-eez please meet your party ..." and the pronunciations seem so idiosyncratic that it is questionable whether Maria and Joaquin will ever connect with their party. The people working and waiting in the food court will sport myriad language sounds as well: The person serving you a cup of coffee or a turkey sandwich might sound very different in Atlanta, "What can I get y'all todaaaaaaeeeee?" and New York, "Whut can I getchuh tuhday?"; then, a six-year-old traveler holds the server and the over-scheduled travelers behind her captive: "I'll have ummmmm ... I'll have ummmmmm ... I'll have, ummmm ... ." The harried person behind her rapidly asks, "Wha da ta?" and it takes a few seconds to realize he just asked, "What's the time?"

In one sense, none of the sound distinctions described above are "meaningful," in the sense of forming different words. "Wa da ta" and "What's the time" mean the same thing. Joaquin Paredes and Jo-a-quin Parade-eez are the same person. From another perspective, however, these kinds of sound differences across people—different ways of pronouncing greetings, names, and words, of asking questions, or, ummmm, holding someone's attention—are critically relevant. These contrasts can become the building blocks for judgments about what a person is like, what they know, or whether they would be a competent student, a good friend, or worthy of renting an apartment. Other sound features, like the rhythm of pauses, the placement of umms, and contrasts in intonation can give impressions (or false impressions) about an individual's intentions or personality.

Traditional sociolinguists have characterized how sound contrasts collect into distinctive and systematic sound differences that mark region, ethnicity, or social status; researchers of second language acquisition have studied the "interference" of first language sounds into the sound system of a new "target" language. But today, in an era of mobility and diversity of communication, sound contrasts more often function as repertoire elements, capable of massively diverse effects, far beyond stereotypic representations of ethnicity or social type, or, in the case of language learners, that ephemeral goal of "native-like" proficiency. In this chapter, I present an alternative way of looking at sound contrasts in communication. Rather than understanding "accent" as a monolithic sound system that we can label as "African American," "Southern," "English," or "Native-like," I propose that we see how distinctive features of any of these illusory monoliths function as repertoire elements. When viewed from a repertoire perspective, categorizing how people sound when they talk in terms of labeled codes like an "English" or "Southern" accent is only a first step of analysis—often an inaccurate one. To understand how such "accents" are relevant to speakers themselves, we must understand how those sounds become functional in a particular context of use within an individual's unique communicative repertoire.

When viewed from a repertoire perspective, the way sounds circulate and function is another specification of the "diversity principle":

> **The Diversity Principle Specification for Sound:** *The more widely circulated a communicatively relevant sound is, the more highly diverse the interactions with it will be.*

While a common belief within sociolinguistics used to be that, with increased mobility and wider distribution of mass media, people would begin to sound more and more alike—male and female versions of Walter Cronkite—this has turned out not to be the case. Instead, sounds have become more distributed, and embedded in a far wider diversity of types of interactions. So, perhaps more people *can* sound like Walter Cronkite if they want to, but they may choose not to. And, any "Walter Cronkite" speech tokens, will likely be embedded in a much more linguistically diverse context than the nightly network news. The musician and hip hop superstar Kanye West, for example, might sound like Walter Cronkite sometimes, a middle-class African American from Atlanta at others, and a hip hop performer of the urban thug persona at others; and sometimes, all these ways of speaking may combine in a single utterance—as in, perhaps, an Ashbery poem (see Chapter 2). President Obama also exemplifies similar speech dexterity (as Alim and Smitherman's book-length analysis (2012) has shown).

This chapter will first illustrate some of the relevant sound features that are candidate repertoire elements for building such varied presentations of self and ways of communicating. Then, I will illustrate how these elements take on a diversity of effects in interaction and how speakers draw attention to their relevance through *metacommentary*. To begin to understand how the relevance of a sound emerges through interaction, let us consider the very first interactions of life: our babies'.

Candidate Repertoire Elements: Developing Awareness of Meaningful Sound Distinctions

Phonetic and Phonemic Contrasts of Babyhood

From the time we are babies, we are making distinctions between sounds—this is how we learn our "mother" tongue. Even before birth, babies are able to make distinctions between the sounds a human makes, other sounds in the world, and the specific voice of their own mothers. As David Crystal writes, a newborn sucking steadily on a monitored teet

> sucks away at a steady rate. When it hears the dog, man, and woman sounds, the sucking speeds up a little bit and then slows down. But when it hears the mother's voice it sucks like crazy! It recognizes her.
>
> *(2010, p. 13)*

Even at just a few hours old—and probably because they have been hearing their mother's muffled voice *in utero*—babies recognize the distinctive sounds of their mother's repertoire. The contrast between sounds of one mother's voice and another's is a matter of discrete sound awareness. This is called *phonetic* difference. The difference between one mother saying "I love you" and another mother saying "I love you" may be measurable in an acoustic phonetics lab and detectable by those mothers' babies, but it would not mark the difference between one language and another, or between one word or another in the same language.

There is a crucial difference between sounds as elements of an individual's repertoire—like the precise tone of a mother's voice—and those sounds that are systematically part of a language. Babies might recognize the sound of their mother's voice *in utero*, but they are not born recognizing the sounds of their native language. It takes at least six months of living among speakers of a given language to be able to detect those sound contrasts that make different words have distinct meanings in that language. Some sound contrasts, like the difference between "Light" and "Right" in English, can take five or six years to master (Locke, 1995). An adult raised in an English-speaking household would recognize "right" and "light" as two different words; an adult raised in a Japanese-speaking household would not hear the difference. These language-specific contrasts are called *phonemic* contrasts. Recognizing which of those differences are relevant contrasts is specific to the language a baby's caretakers are speaking. Part of learning to communicate involves sorting out phonetic from phonemic sound distinctions in a given language.

Phonetic and Phonemic Contrasts Beyond Babyhood: Linguistic Profiling

Phonemic and phonetic contrasts are not only part of first language acquisition, they are also what we hear when we recognize the differences between how people speak in different regions or sound like characteristic demographic groups or like "non-native" speakers of languages they have learned as an adult. Some systematic phonemic "regional contrasts" have little impact on meaning: A Bostonian "Pahk the Caaaah" has no alternate meaning from "Park the Car." "Pahk" is not a word with its own distinct meaning in English. It is simply another way of saying "Park." Analogously, people in Philadelphia may drink "AREnge" juice before heading out to an "IGGles'" Game. They sound like they are from Philadelphia, but we still know they are drinking orange juice and watching the Eagles.

Sometimes, however, regional accents involve phonemic contrasts that affect meaning. In these cases, the sound distinctions form different words. For example, during the first few days of living in the state of Georgia, USA, having never lived in the South before, I found myself searching for "pins" for my office bulletin board. As I was looking through an office supply closet, I asked an office assistant, "Where are the pins?" She answered that they were on the right side of the closet. Seeing no pins at all on the right, I was momentarily mystified. Then I saw what was on the right: Boxes and boxes of PENS. For me, the sound difference between "Where are the pins?" and "Where are the "pens" was clearly audible. But, for many Southerners the "I" sound in "pin" and the "E" sound in "pen" have converged. These two words sound identical to speakers of a certain variety of Southern American English. E/I are phonemic contrasts in one variety of English, but not in another.

Blurring of phonemic contrasts across languages and varieties can potentially lead to these kinds of misunderstandings. But usually context sorts things out. Most languages have "homonyms," after all—words that sound the same but are spelled differently, like deer and dear—and we do not often get confused about them (we do not usually need to ask clarifying questions like, "Did you call me 'dear' or do you really think I am a 'deer'?"). Misunderstandings about things like "pins" and "pens" in the South are rare enough to become funny and notable stories when they actually occur.

While misunderstanding someone's "accent" might have to do with these kinds of phonemic blurs, usually, when people correct us, or draw attention to a different way of saying things, it is not because we are failing to make those meaningful distinctions. Sometimes it just feels better to have someone pronounce a word the way we are used to hearing it. After the pin/pen mix-up, for example, I found myself saying, "Oh! You thought I said 'Pens'? No, I said 'PINS'." Ridiculously and potentially insultingly, I over-pronounced the offending words to the office assistant who had been trying to help me.

This kind of zealous and explicit re-pronunciation illustrates that, often, content of the message is not the issue. Just as a baby, unable to decipher any language "content," will recognize a mother's voice and respond with enthusiasm, an adult will recognize someone who sounds like them—or someone who does not. And, almost impulsively, we take note of, and even draw attention to, those differences. We may even feel the need to correct them, to re-pronounce words or phrases for them, to emphasize the distinctions, not to disambiguate the content of the message, but to re-articulate what sounds "right" to us.

While my encounter with the office person in Georgia was hardly harrowing, and even a little entertaining, sometimes an affinity for our own language sounds can take a more harmful turn. This occurs when certain emblematic sounds become attached to categorical judgments about "the other." John Baugh (2003) has coined the word "linguistic profiling" to describe this process, making the analogy to "racial profiling." Racial profiling is usually used to describe how phenotypically black or brown individuals are treated with suspicion solely on the basis of their skin color. The phrase "driving while black," as if it were a crime, sardonically describes the process of racial profiling, pointing out that for many black individuals, simply being black and at the wheel of a car seems to be grounds for police suspicion and, at times, can lead to harassment.

Like racial profiling, Baugh points out that "linguistic profiling" applies to those speakers of varieties of English that seem "black" or "Latino," and he has shown that, simply on the basis of the sound of one's voice, people can be denied access to basic justice in the courts, or to equal treatment in the marketplace. To illustrate how speaking "Professional" or "White" English affords privileges, he describes his own attempt to secure an apartment in Palo Alto, California:

> During all calls to prospective landlords, I explained my circumstances … always employing my "professional voice," which I am told "sounds white." No prospective landlord ever asked me about my "race," but in four instances I was abruptly denied access to housing upon arrival for my scheduled appointment. Although I suspected that these refusals were directly the result of my race, which was confirmed through visual racial profiling, my standard English fluency was (and is) such that I escaped the "linguistic profiling" because I sounded white.
>
> *(2003, p. 159)*

While Baugh is a linguist, who has studied the systemic nature of language differences, and I have heard him give virtuoso performances of any number of

English varieties based on his intimate knowledge of their systemic variation, the kind of discrimination that is involved in linguistic profiling hardly hinges on such detailed knowledge or performances of language varieties or accents. In fact, in his research with the Fair Housing Bureau, Baugh and colleagues found that people can make distinctions simply on the basis of how people on the phone say the word "Hello" (Purnell, Isardi, & Baugh, 1999). In their experiments, they found that, with 80% accuracy, individuals on the phone could label callers black, Latino or white, upon hearing this one word. And, unfortunately, following those judgments, black and Latino callers were often denied renter's insurance.

So, linguistic profiling like this is usually not centered on issues of meaningful, systematic phonemic contrasts. Just as racial profiling is often based on an emotionally fueled fiction of a black/white binary, linguistic profiling is based on similarly emotionally based ideas about good/bad speech. When people do not rent an apartment or provide insurance to someone on the phone because that person "sounds black," they are not denying that person because they did not understand the content of that person's speech. It is not as if the prospective renter used the word "pen" and the landlord thought they were saying "pin." On the contrary, linguistic profiling occurs on the more visceral level of sound distinctions—sometimes phonetic distinctions so subtle they need to be measured in an acoustic phonetics lab to be consciously registered. Yet, everyday people recognize these fine distinctions unconsciously, the same way a baby's finely tuned ears recognize the sound of their own mother's voice. And, as Baugh points out, "On the basis of our keen auditory skills as a species, I believe linguistic profiling will exist as long as human language exists" (Baugh, 2003, p. 166).

So, phonetic contrasts (like the differences a baby hears between two different mothers' voices) and phonemic contrasts (like those that make it possible for English, but not Japanese speakers to distinguish the word "right" from "light") are potential repertoire elements. And, it seems that, in terms of their function within a repertoire, phonemic relationships, while more wedded to a language system, are less important than discrete and emblematic phonetic bits. The sound of an "alien" way of speaking can register in a split second—I know that person said "I love you," but she is definitely not my mother! One does not need to do a detailed sociolinguistic analysis of the phonemic system of a language variety to recognize its functional effects. Speakers generally do not know details about the systematic nature of varieties of speech, but they do react in often-disarming ways to certain emblematic, yet subtle, sound distinctions.

Rhythm and Intonation Contrasts of Babyhood

Another candidate set of sound contrasts—differences in rhythm and intonation—is perhaps even subtler than the distinctions in pronunciation described above. This distinction also emerges in early babyhood. In addition to phonemic and phonetic distinctions, babies are learning how rhythm and intonation function in communication. Long before babies are learning the sound contrasts between "light" and "right," they have begun to sound like native speakers of their own language. This is because they have developed a characteristic rhythm and intonation. As Crystal writes:

> If we mixed up audio-recordings of nine-month-old English, French, and Chinese babies, and asked people to identify where they came from, they could do it. The English-learning babies are beginning to sound English. The French ones are beginning to sound French. And the Chinese ones are beginning to sound Chinese. We can hear a rhythm and intonation that sound familiar.
>
> *(2010, p. 11)*

A canonical rhythm in the English language, for example is iambic. That is, unstressed syllable followed by stressed syllable, unstressed STRESSed, unstressed STRESSed, and so on, as in Hamlet's, "To BE or NOT to BE," or the more everyday "Please CALL me WHEN you GET a CHANCE." Long before English-speaking babies can say these words, they will babble this rhythmic pattern: Ma MA ma MA ma MA ma MA. And, they will sound like they are "talking" in a characteristic English-speaking way. To "sound like" the speaker of another language, babies will develop rhythmic babbling specific to those languages.

Similarly, in those first nine months, babies will develop characteristic intonation patterns. In many English-speaking communities, a request might be signaled with rising intonation, as in, "ma↑ma"; a summons may feature extended vowel sounds: "MaaaaaaaaMaaaaaaaaaa!"; a delighted discovery or a welcome greeting might feature falling intonation: "↑Ma↓ma!" These intonation patterns, like the rhythms of stressed and unstressed syllables, will make a baby "sound" like their caretakers and help them communicate in a given language, even before they are able to say any recognizable words in that language.

Rhythm and Intonation Contrasts Beyond Babyhood

Rhythm and intonation, it turns out, are also crucial to navigating successful communication long into adulthood. Knowing how to pause, and when others will pause, when to jump in, and what sort of intonation to use when jumping in, can be as, if not more important than "native-like" pronunciation when navigating complex communicative territory.

John Gumperz (whose research on *crosstalk* was discussed in Chapter 1) called these patterns of intonation and stress "contextualization cues" and compiled many examples of how Pakistani or Indian speakers stressed certain syllables or used intonation patterns characteristic of Indian English speakers in London, but unfamiliar to Anglophone monoglot Londoners. This research illustrated how, despite mastery of "English," certain rhythm and intonation patterns of Hindi/

Urdu were maintained and, as a result, despite no explicit differences in the content of a message, misunderstandings about the speakers' intent often ensued. In a movie entitled *Crosstalk* (1976), Gumperz illustrated how Anglo British speakers of English, like bank tellers or social workers, often interpreted Indian English-speaking Londoners as pushy, even when the encounters were nearly identical to those more "polite"-seeming encounters they had with other Anglophone monoglot English speakers.

Patterns of rhythm and intonation in classrooms can also critically affect how some students participate or fail to participate. Fred Erickson has studied the rhythm of questions and answers in classrooms to understand how some students manage to get turns and others are continually silenced, despite the desire to participate. Carefully timing the ebb and flow of teacher questions in classroom recordings, Erickson used musical scores to mark the detailed timing and pitch variation of classroom discussions. In this way, he documented how certain adept students (he called them "turn sharks") were able to anticipate precisely where a teacher's questions would end, and jump in just ahead of anyone else who might have wanted to answer. Those who were left speechless were, not surprisingly, those students who were new to English language classrooms—proficient in English, but not with the nuances of intonation necessary to navigate the turn-shark infested interactional waters of a classroom "discussion" (Erickson, 1996).

Even between "native" speakers of English, patterns of rhythm and intonation can dramatically affect opportunities. Erickson investigated this with Jeff Shultz in the study, *Counselor as Gatekeeper*, mentioned in Chapter 1. In high-stakes counseling interactions, in which counselor and student are attempting to negotiate a student's course of study and future career, it turns out that finding common ground—or establishing *comembership*, as they named it—would lead to the counselor taking a more invested advocacy role for the student. However, to find common ground involved a much more nuanced exchange than simply sharing an academic transcript and stating one's career goals. During the first two minutes of the interaction, a delicate interplay of turn-taking and shifts in intonation, pausing and filled pauses, would lead to the discovery of points of comembership (such as shared interests, common backgrounds or the same alma-mater) that would establish a counseling session favorable to the student's concerns. If comembership was not established, the counselor would generally take up a more rigid institutional stance toward the student's needs.

So, for Indian English speakers in London, for English language learners in U.S. schools, and for college students negotiating their future in counseling sessions, picking up on patterns of rhythm and intonation and responding accordingly prove vital to sustaining communication. Babies latch on to the patterns of rhythm and intonation of their caregivers the same way they seamlessly acquire the sound system of the language around them; then, as adults, they hold fast to these patterns. These patterns of rhythm and intonation become part of their communicative repertoire, as much as the more explicitly measurable grammar and vocabulary of the languages they have learned. These repertoire elements can be used strategically—to grab a turn in a classroom discussion, or to establish common ground with a counselor—or they can become liabilities—as when others misunderstand an Indian English speaker's intentions based on his intonation, when a language learner is silenced in class discussion, or when a student fails to win the empathy of her college counselor.

To summarize, phonetic and phonemic contrasts, as well as contrasts in rhythm and intonation are candidate sound distinctions for one's communicative repertoire. Usually phonetic contrasts are negligible and make no difference in meaning, while phonemic contrasts can lead to meaningful contrasts between words: "Pin" and "pen" are two distinct words, but they might be pronounced the same way by a speaker of a Southern variety of English. Still, the kinds of communicative impact sounds have is more often about the more visceral distinctions people make between the sounds they are used to and the way others say things than differences in meaning distinguished solely by phonemic contrasts. Similarly, patterns of rhythm and intonation rarely affect the content of an utterance, but they can affect how someone participates in a discussion, the impression they give, or what people think about them.

Metacommentary: A Way of Drawing Attention to Communicatively Relevant Sound Distinctions

Distinctive accents, intonations or rhythms of speaking can have significant effects on how we judge people and who we choose to communicate with. But, given that these sound distinctions are often so small as to barely register in a speaker's awareness, how do we know which sounds are meaningfully distinctive? How do we know what contrasts are communicatively relevant in a given situation?

In the past, institutional definitions have largely influenced how we describe language. Disciplinary linguistics made a point of sorting languages into codes and defining a speaker of two codes as being "*bi*lingual" (as discussed in Chapter 2). Sociolinguistics has specialized in identifying the sounds of languages that systematically vary across space or social setting. And, despite a growing body of literature on the wide variations in World Englishes and their functional efficacy (Graddol, 1997, 2006), Second Language Acquisition research has focused largely on the relative success in acquiring a "native-like" sound system of a target language. In these disciplinary traditions, the focus has been on how forms become linguistically identifiable parts of a monolithic language whole, be it a regional variety, a formal register, or a "native-like" sound system of a target language.

Traditional sociolinguistic characterizations of language variation have documented small distinctions, with the goal of making generalizations about how groups of people speak. But these top-down, descriptive methodologies cannot account for the relative importance of some sound distinctions, and the irrelevance of others. Some empirical sound distinctions, while statistically significant to sociolinguists, simply do not matter much to some speakers, while they might be noticeable to others. A repertoire perspective illuminates how such small distinctions in sound function for individuals in highly variable and idiosyncratic ways.

But, how do we know what matters and what does not? John Baugh's research illustrated that one way we can tell is when a person does not get to rent an apartment. But often variations in sound, just like the variations in language discussed in Chapter 2, function with more nuance—be it positively or negatively, whimsically or ironically—to include or exclude, or to indicate infinite shades of possibility. One way to find which distinctions are meaningful to speakers, and how, is to look at participants' *metacommentary* on the sounds of language. That is, by noticing the comments interactional participants themselves make about language sounds, we learn about what those sounds mean in that interaction. Usually participants point out distinctive sounds not to characterize sociolinguistically defined varieties or departures from them, but to identify those features that have a communicative impact in the moment.

Metacommentary on the Sounds of Language: The "Aha" Moment

Drawing attention to distinctions in how people pronounce words or the way they say a sentence happens every day. Already, I have given an example of my own metacommentary on the office assistant in Georgia: "Oh! You thought I said 'Pens'? No, I said 'PINS'." That instance illustrates a certain typical metacommentary on "accent," which I call the "Aha" moment. The zealous Aha moment can be an obvious way of calling abrupt attention to the distinct sounds of another person's language.

Metacommentary on the Sounds of Language: Impersonation of Speakers of Other Languages

Another common way of relating to the different sounds of another person's language through metacommentary is the impersonation. Because it is so hard to describe how someone differs from us in the sound of their language, people often illustrate the difference by imitating what another voice sounds like to them.

In the following excerpt, for example, recorded by an international graduate student, students good-naturedly compare the sounds of "Korean speakers" and "Chinese speakers" by talking about how they "make fun" of each other. The languages of "Korean" and "Chinese" are invoked, but the commentary is not on what those languages mean or how to translate them or on any systemic (phonemic) sound differences, but on the emblems of pronunciation that mark speakers of those languages:

SI ME DA

Student 1:	Do you know how we make fun of Korean in Chinese? We end every sentence with "si me da."
Friends A&B:	Haha, si me da. Yeah.
Friend A:	Is this delicious si me da?
Student 1:	Mike you are so young si me da.
Friend B:	You guys are always saying "zhe ge zhe ge zhe ge" and "na ge na ge na ge" in Chinese.
Student 1:	We say "zhe ge" more than "na ge."
Friend B:	"zhe ge" more than "na ge"?
Student 1:	Yes.

Student 1, who recorded this conversation, described these speech tokens as "different ways to make fun of each other's native language." And yet neither "zhe ge" nor "na ge" has a paraphrasable meaning in English (the student later suggested their similarity to "like" and "you know"). These phrases are salient here because they sound distinctive to speakers of other languages—like Korean. Moreover, the "Korean" token, "si me da" is not even an actual word or phrase in Korean. According to Student 1, it is a made-up word that some people use to describe how Korean sounds "in their heads." Other Korean speakers describe it as fragments of respect vocabulary. In this interaction, however, metacommentary marks it as an emblem of Korean-ness—a way others see and hear sounds of their Korean international-student peers around them. For these 20-somethings, from Korea and China, living in Philadelphia, the sounds of Korean and Mandarin—in this case, not the system of the language or a literal translation of these elements—are the salient elements marking their conversations as Korean- or Chinese-sounding.

Metacommentary on the Sounds of Language: Impersonation of the Rhythm and Intonation of Language

Impersonations can also emphasize those contrasts in rhythm and intonation that may be hard to describe analytically, but which are easy, even entertaining, to impersonate. While working with bilingual teachers in Georgia, USA, in the early 2000s, for example, I would frequently hear stories of their interactions with monolingual colleagues and administrators in which these colleagues marked not their Spanish, but their accented English as communicatively relevant. One form this metacommentary would take would be repeated emphasis on misunderstanding accented speech and "aha" moments like this one when someone finally understood a speech token that departed from the typical English-speaking iambic rhythmic pattern (Rymes, Cahnmann, & Suoto-Manning, 2008). Here, in a role-playing activity we created for bilingual teachers, Laura re-enacted her memory of this scene with an administrator:

OH! EEEEE-mail

Admin: Are you aware of the meeting today?
Laura: Yes, I sent you an e-MAIL.
Admin: Excuse me?
Laura: Did you get my e-MAIL?
Admin: Um. I'm sorry?
Laura: Did you get my E-MAIL?
Admin: Oh!! EEEEEE-mail!

The teachers, many of whom were the only Spanish-English bilingual adults at their schools, all empathized with this scenario. In this example, Laura's initial pronunciation of "e-mail," with the stress on "MAIL," gave her utterance a distinctly "non-native" flavor. In the way these teachers played this scene, the word "e-mail" was easy to decipher, but the stress was noticeably different from that of a native speaker of English, and this was apparently what the English-monoglot administrator insisted on drawing attention to.

This brief misunderstanding seems to have little to do with indecipherable phonemic distinctions. Instead, the administrator seemed to be jarred by the stress pattern Laura was using. Finally, when the administrator made sense of Laura's use of the word "e-mail," as depicted here in the re-enactment, she emphatically stressed the more native-like English stress pattern—EEEE-mail. As the teachers role-played this scene, their ironic deployment of stress here (EEEEEE-mail!) illustrated the administrator's own annoyingly clear and, as a consequence, insulting enunciation of a simple English word.

Later, when the bilingual teachers discussed these types of encounters, rather than focusing on the potential insult in this kind of encounter, they emphasized the advantage they held over these monoglot co-workers who simply did not have experience hearing a variety of sounds around them—experiences that these teachers, variously from Cuba, Colombia, Mexico and Venezuela, but now living in the USA, and teaching in Georgia, certainly did. Their metacommentary emphasized an awareness of their more expansive repertoire.

However, it is not always "non-native" speaker talk that draws metacommentary. In other cases, the accented speech of "white people" can be the relevant category for metacommentary. In the example below, a Liberian high school student in Philadelphia, describes being not interested in dating white people because of the *way* they speak English:

FRUSTRATING AND ANNOYING

Janetta: I probably wouldn't date a white guy. It can be hard to talk to white people. ((*She mimics what sounds like forced speech.*)) It becomes frustrating and annoying.
Bill: ((*Laughs and shakes his head.*))

Here, Janetta seems to be drawing attention to subtle contrasts of rhythm and intonation that are hard to describe, and more effectively conveyed through impersonation. She does not say it is hard to talk to white people because you cannot understand them. She simply gives a quick imitation of how their speech has a certain rhythm and intonation that she finds "frustrating and annoying." And Bill, also Liberian, seems to recognize the impersonation, shaking his head and laughing.

So, the Korean and Chinese university students, the bilingual teachers in Georgia, and the Liberian high school students in Philadelphia all spontaneously comment on the unique rhythm and intonation patterns of language around them. As such they recognize and deploy sounds of language as elements of a communicative repertoire. Their impressions of the sounds of others' language are based on tokens of rhythm and intonation, or the sounds of stock phrases such as the Mandarin-sounding "zhe ge." As these impersonations indicate, speakers are not concerned with how these sounds fit into a monolithic system that could be characterized as "non-native" or a "Chinese accent" or "White speech." Rather, in conversation and through metacommentary, these individuals are working out what these sounds communicate in a given interaction—are they offensive, uptight emblems of foreignness or proud identifiers of peer group membership? These sounds are negotiated for their meaning *in situ* and what each sound comes to mean is both highly visceral and contingent on a given context.

New Methods for Identifying Meaningful Contrasts: Citizen Sociolinguists

These examples of metacommentary on the sounds of language also point to a new direction for the field of sociolinguistics. For decades, sociolinguists, using their linguistic and methodological expertise, have compiled data to statistically identify regional varieties. These sound distinctions are compiled as representative models of how people vary in statistically significant ways across regions. Collected into linguistic atlases, these studies document specific borders between, for example, the region where "pin" and "pen" are distinct sounding words, and the region where "pin" and "pen" sound the same. While these atlases might seem like compendiums of arcane trivia to many conversationalists, as the examples above begin to illustrate, everyday speakers nevertheless are highly aware of, care about, and even document, through metacommentary, the functionally important sound contrasts between the varieties they speak and hear. While commentary on "si me da" or "na ge" might not be as detailed characterizations as those compiled within the covers of a linguistic atlas, they are the most relevant and emblematic contrasts of the people who interact with Chinese- and Korean-speaking international students in the United States.

Increasingly, everyday people are compiling more detailed metacommentaries about the sounds of language via Facebook posts, tweets, and other social media, or on YouTube. These postings of everyday metacommentary function somewhat like the more formal "linguistic atlases," compiled by professional sociolinguists. Like "citizen scientists" who have been enlisted to tag migrating butterflies, monitor their own cholesterol intake, or try out behavioral games on their dogs, these "citizen sociolinguists" have become collectors of sociolinguistically meaningful distinctions—meaningful because these are the distinctions that have stood out to everyday people.

Such "citizen sociolinguists" have begun to post detailed metacommentaries on speech varieties by documenting the distinctions they notice in everyday encounters. These descriptions often focus on nuances of rhythm and intonation and, while they are not compiled in published linguistic atlases, they do circulate widely via impersonations posted on the internet in places like YouTube. One example shows people in Philadelphia "properly" pronouncing Street Names in the City (http://www.youtube.com/watch?v=Dd7x9s1-zdk). Each excerpt flashes the Street Sign, and then shows ordinary people using the name, authoritatively pronouncing it the way it "should" be said. For example, two women interviewed confidently enunciate the way to say "Passyunk Avenue":

[Street sign showing Passyunk Avenue is shown]

Woman #1: (*very serious*)	The name of the street is **Pashunk** and Moore.
(*camera cuts to another woman*)	
Women #2: (*smiling confidently*)	**Pashyunk** Avenue.

Here, these women, as the other people in the video, provide information no dictionary could offer, and yet, their voices are certainly no less authoritative (though slightly inconsistent with each other).

In other cases, YouTube also contains a vast compendium of more detailed and nuanced descriptions of ways of speaking. The linguistic anthropologist Angela Reyes (2013), for example, has illustrated how Filipino youth have documented the "Conyo" style of speaking via YouTube impersonations. These citizen sociolinguists attempt to isolate particular rules about "how to speak" like a Conyo, and they impersonate Conyo speakers to illustrate those rules, as in this illustration of "Rule #7" on "How to Speak Like a Teenage Conyo" (http://www.youtube.com/watch?v=s2XAX5EyYSA):

RULE #7: PROLONG SAYING BASIC WORDS (Transcript adapted from Reyes, 2013)

So, liiiiike,
I had a good tiiiime?
But then, liiiike,
I had to leaeeve?

When they, like, started fightiiiing?
'Cause, liiiike,
it got awkwaaaard?
Liiiike,
for meeee?

Conyo is loosely described as a mixture of Tagolog and English, but as the YouTube impersonations illustrate, acting like a "Conyo" involves a much more detailed and nuanced blend of repertoire elements, which Reyes calls a "hybrid bundle." Each of these impersonations then, illustrates those elements of that hybrid bundle that are most relevant for the community of speakers that care about being a "Conyo" or characterizing people this way.

While YouTube impersonators, or "citizen sociolinguists" are obviously not trained professionals, the representations of repertoire that they present are, arguably, just as valid as sociolinguistic descriptions. Moreover, these citizen sociolinguists come up with descriptions that then circulate widely among people who are likely to reproduce these ways of speaking among their peers. Speaking like a "Conyo" then becomes layered with the nuances of the social groups within which this description circulates. (The same is true of impersonations of a "Valley girl," a "Philadelphian," an "English accent," or someone from Brooklyn, all of which—and many more—have video samples on YouTube.) YouTube followers can reinforce or negate particular renditions of these varieties of speech through their own metacommentaries—on YouTube, other social media, or in the real world.

Just as a language learner is more likely to search the web than a language textbook for sociolinguistic information about a simple translation (like "Happy Birthday!"), a teenager curious about Filipino youth culture is more likely to check the YouTube "how to" videos, than an arcane sociolinguistic atlas. When someone wants to know what a "Conyo" or a "person from Philly" or a "person from Brooklyn" speaks like, these web-circulated descriptions are readily available. Do you want to know how kids talk around you and what that means *to them*? Googling, "how to sound like I'm from South Philadelphia" is more likely to give you relevant answers than a trip to the Penn Library. These vast YouTube repositories of metacommentary on language are another form of *participatory culture* (discussed in Chapter 1). Just as the participatory encyclopedia Wikipedia identifies relevant knowledge via grass roots participation rather than a rigidly top-down editorial process, YouTube has created a wealth of information about how people talk, providing a repository for the ideas and impersonations created by new and youthy "citizen sociolinguists."

The special value of the citizen sociolinguists' metacommentary comes not from the empirical reality of any generalizations they make—a professional sociolinguist might do better at this—but the particularities and the attitudes about those particulars they call our attention to. These particularities—the lilty vowel attenuation of a "Conyo" describing a party that "got awkwaaaard?" or the pronunciation of a certain street name in Philadelphia, or the "si me da" of a Korean international student—are then elements that become part of one's repertoire, ready for recycling, or transforming. These are not encapsulated descriptions, published for posterity. Rather, they are snapshots of possibility for what individuals do and can do with language—and what will get noticed.

Indeed, as Rob Moore (2011b) has pointed out, in his research on Irish metacommentaries on accent, whether such metacommentaries are accurate "descriptions" of what gets heard may be beside the point. Rather hard to empirically pin down, the reports collected and the impersonations performed by what I am calling "citizen sociolinguists" are, rather, their own social "practices of reported speech" (p. 44), significant not necessarily for their first order empirical documentation of accent, but their second order reflection of people's strong beliefs about accent and the sounds of language. Moore's (2011a, 2011b) collection of a vast swath of impersonations of the new and fancy Irish accent labeled "D4"—a social analog in Ireland, to the "Conyo" way of speaking among Filipinos—illustrates precisely this point. Irish citizens, resentful of this new D4 accent and its seeming rebuff to traditional Irish ways of speaking, generally sum it up by imitating it, often in print headlines like this one:

> Do you fancy a "point" at the "boor"? Ita O'Kelly puts the accent on how we judge people by the way they speak.
>
> *(From Moore, 2011b, p. 51)*

Moore further suggests that even the detailed work of professional sociolinguists might be more of a second order enactment of a set of these lay beliefs about social relationships than a strict first order empirical description of processes of sound change. Just as the citizen sociolinguists zero in on emblematic descriptions of talk and link them to youthy and overly modern, disloyal social types, the professional sociolinguist links his vowel charts of phonological shift, with no empirical justification, to the observation that "young people aspire to an urban sophistication which is divorced from strongly local Dublin life." So, citizen sociolinguists are not simply stand-ins for "real" sociolinguists. As people conversing in the thick of things, they may have perfected the art of the *socio* in sociolinguistics. And, the sociolinguist might do well to call on those citizen sociolinguists to validate his own musings on the causes of change. If we want to understand how sounds of language are functioning and what they say about social relations, it is to the documentation of these informal citizen sociolinguists—in the form of their metacommentary—that we should probably look. (We will return to this methodological suggestion in the final chapter.)

Communicative Repertoire and the Sounds of Language

"You say *tomayto*; I say *tomahto*." As this 1930s' George and Ira Gershwin lyric points out, and as this chapter has emphasized, even small sound differences can be significant enough to "call the whole thing off"! Such strong reactions may have little to do with the content of a message, and everything to do with strongly held attitudes about how it sounds. How somebody says "hello" can make or break one's first impression. As John Baugh (2003) has pointed out, humans have finely tuned ears, and make judgments about each other—negative and positive—on the basis of very small sound distinctions. However, discrimination of the type Baugh's research has illuminated—when, for example someone is denied a rental because he "sounds black" or "sounds Hispanic"—rarely is based on comprehensive understandings of a system of "African American English" or "Chicano English." Language discrimination, or valorization for that matter, happens far more often on the level of emblematic patches of talk, or a single sound, than on huge systems, encoded and understood as languages or dialects or registers.

This recognition about the impact of emblematic linguistic distinctions has implications for how we use findings from sociolinguistic research. For example, nearly 50 years ago, sociolinguists pointed out that something like "African American English" is not a deviation from a super-standard version of English, but a linguistic system with grammatical patterns as predictable as any arbitrarily labeled "standard" English. This was hailed as a breakthrough, legitimizing African American speech at last, and scholars and educators expected this to have a positive impact on the schooling of African American Children (Labov, 1963). Unfortunately, however, while this type of disciplinary production of labels and codes for ways of speaking are often attempts to legitimate those codes, these labels can do just as much to damage the speakers of those codes as help save them. As soon as we label something as a "code," it becomes arbitrarily enforceable as such. People are identified as "sounding black" on the phone or in the courtroom, for example, and negative profiling can follow. These labeled codes, however documentable their reality may be, can swiftly become gathering spots for second order ideas and beliefs *about* those codes and people who supposedly speak them. Despite Labov's revelations about the systematicity of African American English as a code, school children today who "sound black" will not score as well on tests or graduate at a rate even close to their peers who "sound white" (Ladson-Billings, 2001). *These "meta" realities have real impact.*

Naming a code "African American English" and extolling the fact that it has an internally consistent sound system suggests that there is one categorical version of that code, with the implication that there is one type of person who speaks it. Providing a label and a monolithic analysis of that code also creates an illusion that such a code is equally valid interactionally as other codes, erasing the fact, which Baugh also illustrates through the concept of "linguistic profiling," that much more intractable sociocultural norms and systems of discrimination and racism are in place to exclude speakers of African American English, precisely for sounding African American, no matter how pristine and internally consistent something called "African American English" might be.

Categorical definitions can lead to lumping and discrimination on the one hand; they can, on the other hand, cause those who ostensibly do not fit into that category to go unrecognized. Those who speak other versions of that code, or who switch in and out of that code, can become invisible as "authentic" speakers. The richness of what speakers actually do with their repertoire is diminished as departures from a singular categorical description. As Baugh points out, the idea that there is a single "profile" of the way to speak African American English is as fictitious as the idea that there is a single "profile" of "Standard English." Moreover, reifying "African American English" or any other variety as a pristine whole, makes it difficult for us to see how emblematic pieces of such codes circulate widely and can become highly effective in combination with other elements of an individual's communicative repertoire (cf., Alim & Smitherman, 2012). Instead, we can easily end up categorically seeing one code as bad, one as good.

For example, in his essay on linguistic profiling, Baugh emphasizes that sometimes linguistic profiling is a valorizing move—as when people in the USA positively profile an "English" or "French" accent (as opposed to negatively profiling an "African American" or "Mexican" accent). However, these monolithic characterizations fail to account for how micro-elements of any of these illusory monoliths can be effectively used as part of one's repertoire. An identifiable "way of speaking" is inevitably a combination of many ways of speaking, involving a mix of emblematic elements. For example, rule #2 in the "Talk like a Teenage Conyo" video, discussed above, is "Add a little Accent, whether it is American, English, or Australian."

In practice, features of varieties like "African American," "American," "Australian," "D4," or "British" English and other less codified sound features—of tone, rhythm or intonation—combine in infinitely different ways across situations. The performer Kanye West, for example, is well known as a black recording artist. He is also known for his songs critiquing the façade provided by formal education and the fact that he dropped out of college as soon as his music career took off. Less well-known facts include that his mother was a college English professor, and that he grew up in a middle-class neighborhood, speaking, no doubt, a variety of "Englishes." West will use elements of African American English in his songs and these "African American English" tokens are highly valorized—West has been extolled as one of the best rap lyricists alive. When he speaks to kids, he blends his repertoire, including elements of "African American English" with other repertoire features, like the way he said the word "fronting" in the following statement to high school kids, while encouraging them to stay in school:

> "I got A's and B's," West said with a grin when asked about his high school grades. "And I'm not even frontin'."

> *(Moss, 2005)*

Did Kanye West sound "black" when he made this statement to kids, using the word "frontin'"? To many who were there listening, probably. Sociolinguistically (statistically) speaking, the substitution of "in'" for "ing" word-finally is a consistent feature of African American varieties of English. But does this mean Kanye West, the individual, must always speak this way? No. He has an enormously wide-ranging communicative repertoire and he uses it strategically. He may want to avoid the "frustrating and annoying" version of Standard English (as described by Janetta above), even though he is capable of reproducing it; and he does not have to switch into an "English accent" or a "French accent" to be positively profiled.

By taking a repertoire perspective and exploring metacommentary, this chapter has provided a new approach to highlighting the variety of sounds that make up an individual's communicative existence. Selective elements of a repertoire combine to produce effects, not precise reproductions of linguistically described monolithic systems. The same holds true for the sounds of multiple Englishes and non-native Spanishes, Portugueses, etc. Paying attention to the sounds, rhythms and intonations of who we speak with—and drawing on our own repertoire to respond in kind and develop some rapport—is often more important than deciphering a "content" of their speech or naming the "language" or "variety" being used.

Increasingly, communicative nuances circulate via impersonations and metacommentary on the internet. Ten years ago, "How to Talk like a Teenage Conyo" would be an inaccessible mystery for most people. Now, the sounds and nuances of infinite varieties stream to us through social media, vastly expanding the communicative repertoire of anyone with a computer and a pinch of curiosity. As the next chapter illustrates, YouTube has also expanded the way that popular culture emblems—from Pokemon to Barack Obama—enter our repertoires and take on communicative value.

4

MASS MEDIA AND POPULAR CULTURE[1]

In a primary-school classroom in Georgia, second-graders call out the names of Pokémon characters and burst into laughter. In a live interview on the Al Jazeera news network, several background onlookers in Egypt are wearing New York Yankees caps. On Facebook, a Swedish music producer uses fragments of Aymara, an indigenous language of the Andes, to promote global hip hop. Each of these examples illustrates different ways mass-circulated culture infuses a communicative repertoire. This chapter will unpack and exemplify each of these different processes: (1) how explicit references to mass media function as part of one's repertoire; (2) how mass media provide communicative elements that people incorporate into their overall presentation of self; and (3) how the mass media then further circulate these hybrid identity repertoires.

When people make popular cultural references they automatically select a set of listeners for their talk. The child who calls out the name of a Pokémon character in class, for example, selects his peers, specifically those who are Pokémon fans, as his primary interlocutors. Suddenly the teacher is excluded from the talk in her own classroom. Adult conversation follows the same principles: Mention the author Jonathan Franzen and some adults will perk up, others will look blank. In this way, even simple references to widely circulating popular culture are part of one's communicative repertoire. Finding points of overlap can be crucial. As John Cusack's character realizes, when he falls for a stunningly beautiful singer in the movie *High Fidelity*, sometimes "it's not who you know, it's what you know." This occurs to him when he realizes that, despite his lowly position as a record store owner and her lofty position as a gorgeous and iconic pop singer, she falls for him over conversation, as he reveals his encyclopedic knowledge of music and they discover they have brilliantly overlapping tastes.

But mass-mediated culture also works as part of one's repertoire in more subtle ways. Often, rather than referring explicitly to popular figures, names of songs or movies, etc., people selectively mimic elements of popular personas that are widely circulating. Thus, across the world, people don New York Yankees hats just as they have seen hip hop artists do in videos that circulate, often through YouTube, even to the most remote internet cafés. Similarly, across the USA, countless teens and 'tweens have hair that looks uncannily Justin Bieber-like. Even the way people walk or gesture or punctuate their speech (yo!) often emerge from widely circulated popular sources. Features like these are much more unconsciously incorporated into an individual's communicative repertoire than explicit references to "Justin Bieber" or "Jay-Z," but they can be as effective at selecting a group of people who share common ground (and excluding others who may not).

Finally, these mass-mediated repertoire elements circulate and combine in ways that foster more diverse forms of recognition globally. The Swedish music producer mentioned above, for example, invokes indigenous Bolivian rap while using English, Swedish, and Aymara on his website. His own photo combines obviously Caucasian facial hair with a notably indigenous South American knitted cap. As he exemplifies, individuals never recirculate exact replicas of popular cultural performances, but hybrid forms compiled of diversely recognizable repertoire elements (Swinehart, 2011).

As these examples suggest, common ground with respect to mass-mediated culture is not found through homogenization or "McDonaldization" but through new combinations that foster new forms of repertoire overlap. Consistent with The Diversity Principle, *the more widely circulated and mass-produced a message is, the more highly diverse the interactions with it will be.* This is because these widely circulating forms become incorporated into individuals' *communicative repertoires* to be deployed in indeterminate variation. In this chapter, I will illustrate this point in detail, by first looking at the meteoric rise of the pop artist "Soulja Boy" and his hit, "Crank Dat." Following the illustration of the circulation and recontextualization of Soulja Boy's hit, I apply this method of analysis to a less seemingly trivial mass-mediated movement—Obama's first presidential campaign. By tracing the pathway of semiotic forms as recontextualized and circulated via YouTube, I demonstrate how widely circulating cultural emblems become incorporated into individual-level communicative repertoires.

The concept of *recontextualization* (Baumann & Briggs, 1990) is crucial to our understanding of how popular culture becomes incorporated into an individual's repertoire. In many senses, recontextualization is simply a creative form of recycling cultural elements: We hear a melody, we sing it to ourselves, or our children, or with our friends. We hear a phrase on a TV show—"Legendary!"—and we use it to praise a student's contributions in class discussion. In such instances, we are using these fragments of the cultural surface to add to our repertoire, the same way we might use a word in another language, or a catchy intonation pattern we grew up with.

However, while this kind of cultural recycling is ubiquitous, the precise meanings that evolve when these elements are recontextualized are highly variable. While a single act of recontextualization (e.g., humming a song-lyric to oneself) does not necessarily endure as part of a shared local repertoire, over time, select recontextualizations become recognized as having a certain common communicative value within a social group. A Soulja Boy dance step, for example, may become a repertoire element that functions differently in different social groups. So, because the same semiotic elements take on varied and localized communicative functions, no matter how massively produced and ubiquitously distributed a product is—and no matter the degree of corporate sponsorship—any text contains repertoire elements that are selected for differently by different groups. As such, again, *the more widely circulated and mass-produced a message is, the more highly diverse the interactions with it will be.*

There are practical, even ethical (not simply theoretical) reasons for taking a repertoire approach to understanding mass media and popular culture. Most importantly, by seeing how cultural emblems function as part of an individual's repertoire, we can avoid the potentially essentializing tendencies of mainstream cultural analysis (or market research) that over-generalizes what certain demographic groups do or think (potentially leading to misunderstandings, prejudice, or unfair discrimination). Just as certain language sounds discussed in Chapter 3—"African American English" or "D4" varieties of Irish English or intonation of a Filipino "Conyo" variety of English—may mean very differently in different situations and in combination with other features, popular culture references take up different functions in different groups. As Blommaert (2010) has pointed out, in this age of globalization and super-diversity we just do not know anymore (if we ever did) what generalizations certain semiotic signs—skin color, age, clothing, linguistic code—can be linked to.

So, a repertoire perspective provides a new lens for understanding diversity by bracketing cultural generalizations and, instead, empirically tracing the relationship between widely circulating messages and their infinitely varied deployment by individuals. Just as individuals can use a variety of languages (English, French) or ways of speaking, and blend them creatively to produce infinite effects, individuals can use gestures and clothing styles of pop stars, popular dance steps, ways of speaking, or famous phrases ("Yes We Can!") to enhance their communicative repertoire. I demonstrate this process in the rest of this chapter by examining how widely circulating semiotic forms (a song, a dance, or a phrase) are taken up by individuals as part of their *communicative repertoire* and redeployed in hybrid combinations with relevant repertoire elements common to that individual's social milieu. Rather than relying on *a priori* demographic categories for analysis, this repertoire approach provides a non-essentializing way of investigating difference.

I illustrate this point by first looking at a phenomenon arguably categorized as a "hip hop artist" named Soulja Boy and the meteoric rise of his hit, "Crank

Dat." By looking at how this song has been recontextualized in a fantastic diversity of forms, I want to illustrate that mass media afford both homogenization and infinite recontextualization. Suburban elementary school boys, Harry Potter fans, even MIT professors and their students have performed versions of this song. But they all use it very differently. And, rather than being mindlessly numbed by it, each group, to different degrees, becomes drawn to select recontextualizations which that group recognizes as having a certain common communicative value. In this way, recontextualized elements of the Soulja Boy performance become part of locally functional communicative repertoires.

Both these phenomena illustrate a similar process, and this chapter, ultimately, will illustrate a method for understanding internet-circulated mass media messages and their effects. First, some words on the relationship between recontextualization and repertoire.

Recontexualization and Communicative Repertoire

As discussed in detail in Chapter 1, by *communicative repertoire*, I mean the collection of ways individuals use language and other means of communication (gestures, dress, posture, accessories) to function effectively in the multiple communities in which they participate (Rymes, 2010). In the previous two chapters, I have outlined how both named languages—for example, Spanish or French—and sound variations—such as pronunciation and intonation—function as repertoire elements. In this chapter, I further expand the term to include widely circulating mass-mediated forms like a YouTube-circulated dance step, a cereal brand name like Fruit Loops, or a memorable phrase (Yes We Can!). So, an individual's communicative repertoire includes not only linguistic elements (and, often, multiple languages—*si se puede!*), but also mass-mediated cultural elements, circulated, often, via viral internet sources like videos found on YouTube. Like those individuals Gumperz studied (see Chapter 1), who drew on multiple languages to make their way through communicatively complex marketplace negotiations, people today draw on multiple communicative repertoire elements—both multiple languages and myriad mass-mediated semiotic forms—as they go through their daily routine performing relevant and functional identities.

These repertoire elements are highly recontextualizable bits—because they are often catchy, memorable, or dramatic. Like poetic features such as rhyme or parallelism originally noted as highly recontextualizable by Bauman and Briggs (1990) and Silverstein and Urban (1996), internet phenomena tend to become more widely circulated (and "go viral") when they have salient features that are recognized when reproduced in a new context. However, when deployed in new contexts as part of an individual's unique communicative repertoire, these recontextualized bits also develop new, highly localized, functionality. The significance of a single recontextualization of a viral video feature is impossible to analyze. It could be as potentially meaningless as tapping a rhythm aimlessly on one's office desk. But, when this recontextualization is recognizable by others (as evidenced by, for example, shared opinions about YouTube videos, or exchanged glances across a classroom), it is functioning as part of an individual's locally functional communicative repertoire.

In schools, for example, a certain gesture, phrase or pattern of dress, recontextualized in a classroom interaction, can affect how a child participates in that setting and who count as legitimate interlocutors. Similarly, outside the classroom, every day, we make choices about with whom we interact and how we interact with them based on momentary mentions or enactments of widely circulating emblems of identity. When people make popular cultural references by mentioning a celebrity, wearing their hair in a certain way, or using phrases made famous by stars ("Legendary"), they automatically select a set of listeners for their talk.

Such widely circulating, mass-mediated semiotic forms become recontextualized in an individual's communicative repertoire in special performances (like YouTube videos) and in everyday interaction. The most obvious way people use mass media as a repertoire element is through *explicit reference*. This is exemplified above, when kids mention "Pokémon" or an adult talks about "Jonathan Franzen"; a second way we deploy mass media as part of our repertoire, is through *implicit enactment*, as when we (to varying degrees of awareness) try to act like or emulate the actions or personas of widely circulating types. Someone might, for example, try to look like a Pokémon character, or get their hair cut like Justin Bieber. This kind of creative emulation has been documented (in its more conscious instantiations) by Henry Jenkins and others in their studies of fan culture (Jenkins, 1992; 2006). But, probably the most common and least obvious way that widely circulating semiotic forms become incorporated into one's repertoire is in *disparate hybrid combinations*, as will be illustrated in this chapter.

In what follows, I illustrate several examples of such disparate hybrid combinations of repertoire elements by analyzing YouTube variations of viral videos. In these variations, elements of YouTube performances become recontextualized in combination with other widely circulating mass-mediated semiotic forms, as part of an individual's communicative repertoire. Even a cursory familiarity with YouTube and its fans reveals that individuals in the same social groupings tend to have sets of YouTube favorites that are largely overlapping. YouTube, while never explicitly designed to be such, has evolved to become a site of participatory culture (c.f., Burgess & Green, 2009) that often converges with face-to-face interaction.[2] For this reason, YouTube can be an ideal context to study social connections that otherwise remain largely invisible, particularly the combination and recombination of repertoire elements that create meaningful performative acts. This chapter begins to illustrate how we might usefully engage with this medium to learn generally about social and communicative processes and, more specifically, how youth use widely circulating media iconography to engage with each other and the (digital) world.

The Crank Dat Soulja Boy Story

In January, 2006, DeAndre Cortez Way, age 15, (soon to become known as Soulja Boy), opened a YouTube account and started posting song and dance videos he made in his father's home in Batesville, Mississippi (pop. 8,000). A little over a year later (March, 2007), his song, "Crank Dat" was on mainstream radio, and in another month, Michael Crooms, also known as Mr. Collipark of Collipark Music (an imprint of Interscope), met with Soulja Boy and gave him a recording contract.

In the official YouTube video version of the song and dance that resulted, Mr. Collipark himself is depicted as a latecomer to the massive success of Soulja Boy, who initially vaulted himself to fame via viral internet-based mechanisms. In this self-designated "official" video, Mr. Collipark is shown using the same online mechanisms to sign Soulja Boy that kids around the country had been using to access Soulja Boy's music for months.[3]

From its humble beginnings in Batesville, Mississippi, this song was catapulted, largely via YouTube and MySpace to massive commercial success. As such, it easily falls into the category of marketized hip hop sell-out. Thanks to YouTube and downloadable Ring Tones, this song could be scapegoated as the pinnacle of "monolithic homogenized consumer taste" (Barber, 2008, p. 290). But the life of "Crank Dat Soulja Boy" extends far beyond this official version. The same vehicles that enable this song/dance to be massively distributed have also allowed it to be massively re-embedded in new and varied communicative repertoires. There are far more YouTube video recontextualizations of "Crank Dat" than there are Soulja Boy hits. And, because of his original use of YouTube and MySpace, Soulja Boy has been able to get his "message" recontextualized in social networks far beyond his partying peers in Batesville, Mississippi, or Mr. Collipark's media domain.

The Variations

If you look up "Crank Dat" on YouTube, you will immediately be drawn to hundreds more videos posted that recontextualize Soulja Boy's hit in widely varied ways. Obvious features distinguish these variations from one another and are listed in Table 4.1. The music and beat, the lyrics, the huge, colorful clothes, the bling, being phenotypically black, being male, even being live (as opposed to animated) are all features of the original song that are played with or left out of the variations. As we go down the list of recontextualizations on the left of Table 4.1, features of the original drop away.

Obviously, the goal of these variations is not to simply emulate the original. Rather, semiotic elements of the *Soulja Boy* performance become recontextualized in the new video variation. Additional elements become incorporated, many of which may also be widely circulated elements. In this sense, all of the variations

TABLE 4.1 Distinctive Features Occurring in Soulja Boy Variations

	Distinctive Features						
Variations	Music	Dance Moves	Live Action	Lyrics	Black	Male	Appurtenances
"Official Web Site" version	+	+	+	+	+	+	+
Three white Boys "original"	+	+	+	+		+	+
Black Girls Version	+	+	+	+	+		
Blonde U of E Cheerleaders	+	+	+	+			
MIT Dancers	+	+	+	+			
Crank Dat Folger Boy	+	+	+		+		
Crank Dat Harry Potter	+	+	+				
Spongebob	+	+		+			
Bambi	+			+			
Cereal	+	+					
Third Graders In Class		+	+				

illustrate how different individuals use *disparate hybrid combinations* of repertoire elements to create a meaningful and unique performance. As elements of the original drop away, elements of the creator's communicative repertoire become more important to the overall performance.

To exemplify this point, at the middle of the list, we have *Folger Boy*: The name itself encapsulates punny hybridity—Folgers Coffee plus Soulja Boy is uniquely absurd. The video is also pervasively hybrid and absurdly hilarious. It preserves the music track, the live action element, and the dance moves, and the performer is black. But the lyrics (very raunchy in the original), while still rhythmically intact, have taken on funny, coffee-oriented content. For example, the line in the original video hit, "You gotta punch then crank back three times from left to right," becomes "you just gotta make a cup and take three sips." The infamous line, "superman da ho" (which I suggest readers Google if not familiar with the use of "superman" as a verb), becomes a slightly more innocent "coffeebean da ho." The arguably exhibitionist "wat me crank it, wat me ro" of the original is now replaced with "wat me drink it, wat me po."[4]

Compared to others on the list, Folger Boy is relatively unknown (with only tens of thousands of views, compared to tens of millions of views of the "official" video) and the third-graders who initially told me about Soulja Boy had never heard of it. (Still, the stodgy old Folgers brand might have done well to take note of this burst of recognition provided by creative consumers!) But other variations, even more distinct from the original have far more viewers. As we go down the cline, and resemblance to the original is further bleached away, wildly popular animated parodies take over. Clearly, popularity is not gained through fidelity to the original (or mindless emulation). Rather, as elements of the original depart, new repertoire elements combine with the remaining Soulja Boy features for new kinds of performative effects.

The massively popular "Bambi" version also illustrates a hybridity of mass-mediated elements. While this video preserves Soulja Boy's lyrics and music, nothing else remains. Bambi voices Soulja Boy's dramatic opening "YOOOOOOOL!" Owl intones, "Soulja Boy Tellem." The other lines are also painstakingly lip-synced by Bambi and other forest friends. This video received over 1 million views before being yanked from YouTube for copyright infringement (Disney images).[5] Disney, apparently, entrenched in traditional copyright paranoia, never hopped on the participatory culture bandwagon or recognized the marketing power of creative consumerism. While this is a unique, highly individual production, its entertainment value depends on viewers who have some familiarity with Bambi, just as the joy of the Folger Boy version depends on some familiarity with Folgers Coffee. Each of these variations depends on a relationship with another widely circulated and mass-produced form, but the combination of the two mass-produced forms yields the highly creative recontextualization.

Further down the list, there are more brand name associations, most notably (for the third-graders), the Captain Crunch variation, in which different cereal spokes-icons flash on the screen (Captain Crunch, of course, but also The Fruit Loops Toucan, Tony the Tiger, "Snap, Crackle, and Pop" from Rice Crispies, and even the kindly old white-haired Quaker oatmeal man). These cereals all get mention in the reworked Soulja Boy lyrics, as in, "Hey what's up man, I got this new cereal for y'all called Cap'n Crunch." This version has received far fewer viewings than the Bambi version (only 230,454) but was a huge hit with the suburban Philadelphia third-graders.[6] This video combines repertoire elements—hip hop register *plus* sugary cereal!—for which these kids have massive affinity.

At the bottom of the resemblance cline, I have listed a barely recognizable version of the dance, containing no additional branded elements, and never posted on YouTube. Instead, this is a version that was periodically performed surreptitiously by third-graders during class. Rather than recombining it into a consumer product repertoire, the boys seamlessly incorporated the Soulja Boy dance into their school-boy repertoire, occasionally performing a silent version of the dance during "seat work" in school, a time when students were allowed to quietly get up and stand next to their desk and stretch, if needed. This performance of Crank Dat was so muted as to be nearly beyond recognition. The teacher never once saw these mini-Crank-Dat dances as disruptive or, the boys speculated, even recognized them as anything other than a sort of idiosyncratic stretching break. The boys' peers, however, knew what was going on, having fully absorbed the moves into their own unique, third-grade-boys-from-suburban-Philadelphia communicative repertoire.

Viewer Response

As the massive range of videos that were spawned by the Soulja Boy dance video illustrate, describing the effects of at least this form of mass media as "one-dimensional" seems inaccurate. Viewers have responded not with passive reverence but with videos of their own. Furthermore, the comments posted on YouTube in response to these remakes also illustrate that YouTubers have not become one-dimensional consumers of whatever is posted on the site, but active critics who revolt at the sign of homogeneity of product or opinion. Moreover, fans are not drawn to certain videos by abstract notions of "quality," but through recognition of the creative recombinations of repertoire elements that appeal to their local sensibilities.

As mentioned above, popularity of videos has little to do with fidelity to the original. In general, the further down the cline you go, the more positive the YouTube commentaries are. At the top of the cline, however, people's remarks about the Official Soulja Boy video are almost universally negative. The comments on the original Soulja Boy video (now gone) framed this as the "hip hop" genre (gone very very bad) and Soulja Boy as a fake, talentless sell-out, a one-hit wonder with nothing to say and no flow. Some comments even accused Soulja Boy of causing the end of hip hop.

Obviously, the song's power is not in its qualities as an artistic whole, but as a widely circulating video with highly recontextualizable features (catchy tune, and easy-to-perform dance steps). As demonstrated, this song has spawned so many imitations that it hardly qualifies as "hip hop" any more. When the hip hop elements of the performance are recontextualized in combination with other repertoire elements, however, comments become much more favorable. Many of the variations, especially those further down the cline of resemblance to the original—Bambi, Spongebob, cereal—are pronounced "the best YouTube video ever" by online commentators.

These favorite variations also indicate the range of communicative repertoires into which elements of the Soulja Boy performance have been absorbed. If you are an older adult who has never gotten into "hip hop" things, but for whom coffee is part of your daily round, and if you remember "Folgers" in your house growing up, you might find "Folger Boy" particularly good. It is also a favorite, apparently, of workers at the Folgers factory. One YouTube commenter on Folger Boy writes:

> hahaha! I'm at the folger's coffee factory in Kansas City. Some of the employees have stumbled on this video and they find it hilarious, including me! Keep on representin that Folgers!
>
> *(YouTube comment from Kimmy4205)*

The phrase "Keep on representin that Folgers!" combining hip hop diction and the stodgy Folgers brand, encapsulates the hybridity of the video itself—the incongruous lifestyle combination of hip hop dress and dance with the drinking of a morning cup of Folgers Coffee. So, Soulja Boy references become part of a more enduring, and locally communicative repertoire for "some of the employees" at the Folger's factory through the recombination of that widely circulating dance with Folgers Coffee.

While Folger Boy had direct appeal to Folger's factory workers, other hybrid combinations of widely circulating mass-mediated cultural emblems have more appeal for different social groupings. The third-grade boys, connoisseurs of both sugary cereals and their brand icons, chose Crank Dat Cereal as their favorite. The third-graders enjoyed recognizing sugary cereals and their animated spokespersons represented. The online comments about this clip echo the boys' appreciation and ooze admiration for this video and the artistry of its creator, Markarel. Many commenters, like the following, also mention that, though they despise the original, they admire this "spoof":

> Great video :D Funny how a spoof about cereal can be better_than the original song.
>
> *(Comment posted by ivallane)*

> I absolutely hate the original, but THIS is HILARIOUS.
>
> *(Comment posted by "DeadBatteryVideos")*

> YESSSSSS i fuckin hate these crank that songs ... buh i admit this is_creative.noyce job!!
>
> *(Comment posted by "stepsz")*

As these examples indicate, as elements of the original Soulja Boy performance drift away, other widely circulating repertoire elements enter into the subsequent recontextualizations. While Folger Boy and Crank Dat Captain Crunch have few of the distinctive features of the original "Crank Dat, Soulja Boy" performance, they have replaced the elements that have been dropped along the way with a new array of repertoire elements relevant to their own cultural projects or peer groups.

Mass Media and Individual Communicative Repertoires

Soulja Boy's song and dance and its viral distribution through YouTube and social networking sites illustrates that, contrary to some fears about the cultural effects of mass circulation of low-brow art, mass media are not a homogenizing, deadening force. Instead, they are a way that highly localized recontextualizations spread exponentially. Today, through e-mail, social networking sites, YouTube, and the internet in general, a range of expressive resources are available for incorporation into individual communicative repertoires. Even a highly consistent mass-mediated message has a panoply of distinctive features that will be recontextualized with other repertoire elements in massively diverse social formations. The result is a huge fan base, but not a homogeneous one. Some might argue that these recontextualizations, while not homogeneous, are perhaps a bit deadening, or at least content-challenged. Perhaps. However, despite the purely entertainment-oriented nature of this Soulja Boy example, this phenomenon is not trivial. In fact, another individual was recently catapulted to the Presidency of the United States thanks, in large part, to this same new-fangled, mass-mediated but highly localized process.

The "Yes We Can" Story

Just about the same time Soulja Boy was signed to Interscope Records, Barrack Obama was beginning his own meteoric rise to the top. This rise can be largely attributed to the same processes that propelled Soulja Boy's fame: viral dissemination of a consistent message, distinctive repertoire elements locally selected for, leading to massive uptake of diverse elements of a message.

On January 8, 2008, shortly after his victory in the Iowa presidential primary, Obama lost in New Hampshire. Despite this loss that day, he captured the mass media with his "Yes We Can" oratory, which was subsequently transformed into a music video by will i. am (of Black Eyed Peas)[7] and recontextualized in massively varied repertoires. Like Soulja Boy, the Obama Campaign, with the help of YouTube and social networking sites, was able to get Obama's "message" recontextualized in a fantastic diversity of new communicative contexts, the wide-ranging specificity of which could never have been predicted by the crafters of Obama's original rhetoric.

The Variations

In Table 4.2, I have listed as distinctive features those causes denoted by the content of Obama's original "Yes We Can" speech—accomplishments that YES WE CAN do or that, in the past, people said YES WE CAN do these things and then did them. So in the original speech, he does mention that we can heal this nation, repair this world, go to the mountaintop (as Martin Luther King did), save our planet, restore opportunity, give women rights, go to the moon, organize workers and bring troops home from Iraq.

TABLE 4.2 Distinctive Features Occurring in *Yes We Can* Variations

	Distinctive Feature/Cause									
Variation	YES WE CAN/ *Si se puede*	Repair this World	Heal This Nation	Go to the Mountain top like MLK	Give Women Rights	Restore Opport unity	Save Our Planet	Go to the moon	Organ- ize Work- ers	Bring the troops home
Original Speech	+/−	+	+	+	+	+	+	+	+	+
Will i. am Original video	+	+	+	+	+	+				
Maria Muldaur Pointer Sisters Mix	+	+	+	+*	+	+	+			
International Multi- lingual version	+	+	+	+	+	+				
Barrackap- pela	+	+	+	+						
Yes We Can Can Pointer Sisters Mix	+	+	+							
No We Can't (McCain)	+	+								
Pro Medical Marijuana Ad	+									
Yes We Can (Bob the Builder)	+									

Proceeding down the left-hand column listing variations, there emerge more and more divergent versions of the original. Just as the Soulja Boy recontextualizers select from and omit various distinctive features of the original "Crank Dat," creators of the different versions of the "Yes We Can" video select from the wide array of causes enumerated in Obama's original "Yes We Can" speech.

Just following the will i. am video, is Maria Muldaur's version. The music and most of the lyrics for this one are taken from the 1970s' Pointer Sisters hit "Yes We Can Can" and, unlike the will i. am version, are not directly dubbed from Obama's speech. Nevertheless, this version includes almost all of the causes mentioned in Obama's original speech and she throws in the "si se puede" reference (made explicit in the will i. am version) with an image of Cesar Chavez. Certainly the Pointer Sisters' allusion and Maria Muldaur's own artistic legacy as a folk singer/songwriter appeal to an older demographic than will i. am's song, which derives from his location in the youth pop world and his heritage as a member of the pop band Black Eyed Peas. Perhaps because of the specificity of the social domain to which Maria Muldaur appeals, Maria Muldaur's "Yes We Can" (though highly produced and professionally arrayed) received only 56,000 or so hits, and quite a few harsh comments.[8]

Videos featuring young people, however, no matter what the video's production values, often become very popular. Farther down the list, for example, we come to "Barrackapella," featuring talented yet scruffy-looking *a capella* singers (all white) from an Oregon college. This version stays very true to Obama's New Hampshire speech. But it also omits mention of many of the causes enumerated by Obama. Still, despite its amateur production values and general simplicity, this clip has received over 400,000 hits and rave reviews.[9]

The subsequent variations listed in Table 4.2 continue to decrease in resemblance to Obama's original speech. The final three on the cline bear least resemblance to the original, and, especially in the case of the legalization ad, seem more about something else. These new versions embed the "Yes We Can" message into new repertoires that diverge widely from the content and the iconography of Obama's original speech: *Si Se Puede* (Spanish for "Yes We Can" and the signature slogan for Cesar Chavez grape boycott) was never part of Obama's original. Nor were legalizing marijuana or supporting gay marriage. Yet, just as Soulja Boy's lyric became part of repertoires that included Fruit Loops and Folgers Coffee, Obama's "Yes We Can" message joins forces with wide-ranging repertoire elements—drug legalization, gay marriage, *Bob the Builder*—in subsequent recontextualizations.

In the drug legalization video, for example, the "Yes We Can" phrase has been recontextualized in a completely new speech event, accomplishing an entirely different form of social action—an award-winning marijuana legalization ad campaign. The YouTube video also became very popular—receiving over 450,000 hits.[10] This legalization issue, though never present in the New Hampshire speech, was also incorporated into the McCain criticism "No You Can't" video, retrospectively making it seem as though Obama included "yes we can legalize medical marijuana" in his original New Hampshire speech, which he did not. This video also negated gay marriage, implying Obama had said "Yes You Can" get married if you are gay—which, at that point, Obama had never said or advocated. This video illustrates how the layering of semiotic features of new social projects and communities gets continually more complex with further distance from the original: "No You Can't!" is both a parody of will i. am's original video and a critique of McCain's negativity. While it may somewhat inconveniently (for Obama) invoke causes implying that Obama endorsed them, it simultaneously, in its critique of McCain, does useful dirty work (negative campaigning) for Obama.[11] This received nearly 2 million views.

The last recontextualization on the list makes the obvious connection between Barrack's "Yes We Can" and the identical *Bob the Builder* slogan (Can we build it? Yes we can!). This is, perhaps the most negative recontextualization of Obama's message. It is also the variation that retains almost no distinctive features of the original. Simply the three words, "yes we can," with the superimposition of Obama's image now and then.[12]

Just like the Soulja Boy variations, these variations take up the original with massively diverse creativity. The recontextualizations are not simply mindless imitations of the original: There are no videos of people trying to copy, exactly, Obama's speech and his delivery. Each of these is an active response to the original message, yet each depends on the original message for its content to matter. Moreover, each message further disseminates the original message, re-embedding it in new social domains. In this way, Obama was able not only to spread his message, but also to re-embed it in the communicative repertoires of groups—gay marriage supporters, drug legalization types—he never explicitly supports. In this way, his message was perfect, not for its content, but because it was easily recontextualizable in the communicative repertoires of subgroups who may otherwise have been less attracted to him. Young people, for example, or gay men, or those who want to legalize marijuana.

Conclusion and Implications

I have described a process for understanding the effects of a mass-mediated message. Even the most widely circulated (viral) mass-mediated message is not one that is repeated identically by mindless drones. Rather, these examples have illustrated how, by rethinking the micro/macro dichotomy in terms of recontextualization and repertoire, we are able to trace empirical pathways through which semiotic forms gain differential functional value as they are embedded in new communicative repertoires. The process goes like this: A video circulates on YouTube. Individuals re-make that video—not replicating it, but highlighting certain semiotic elements by recontextualizing them in a new semiotic array. In this new hybrid combination, the individual makes a bid at recognition by like-minded peers. In this way, the individual is using the recontextualized bit as a new element of his already established communicative repertoire.

This is a process that also occurs without YouTube. Imagine a sixth-grade peer group. They always greet and take leave in certain ways (Yo, what's up? Let's roll!), they wear similar clothing (big shorts and t-shirts), and share certain hobbies (skateboards and comics), food tastes (energy drinks), and ideologies (they belong to green club, recycle, and would never litter). These are relatively stable elements of this peer-group repertoire. But there are always elements entering into it and being subtracted. One day, someone hears the word "snap!"—maybe on a TV show, maybe in a commercial, a song, or a conversation his big brother was having. Who knows? But he remembers it and he wants to use it. He could try it once, while hanging out, realizing he is running late and needs to leave immediately: "Snap! Let's roll!" His friends get it. He has recontextualized this word.

But is that word now part of his communicative repertoire? This depends on whether it is functional and recognizable. Do his friends recognize it and show its legitimacy by using it themselves. Does it fill a communicative niche? Soon all the group uses "snap." "Snap! I forgot my lunch." "Snap! My mom's here!" Gradually they get what it means, while creating what it means—in their group. Snap! Across multiple interactions, embedded in a shared semiotic array, "snap" becomes a functional repertoire element—not simply a word from somewhere else that is momentarily recontextualized in these kids' talk. The value of "snap" in this peer group—just like the value of speaking "D4 Irish," "British English," or "French"—draws on both widely circulated mass media cachet as well as its local functionality.

Obviously, this process—recontextualization and incorporation into local communicative repertoires—occurs without YouTube, but YouTube is a remarkable medium because it makes this process visible to the analyst. Just as a photographer's developing fluid suddenly reveals a previously invisible image in the darkroom, the medium of YouTube reveals and accelerates (and extends globally) social processes that have, until now, been largely invisible to us as discourse analysts worried about micro and macro. YouTube's original design was highly underdetermined. YouTube's current organization, as a site that features exponentially compounding response videos, bloomed from the way many users pushed the site, through their own practices on the site, to be a medium for social interaction and sharing (Burgess & Green, 2009).

Because YouTube evolved in this way into a site of chained response videos, it reveals even more clearly the continual recontextualization of semiotic elements in local repertoires: An Obama video is posted and the phrase "Yes we can" begins to circulate. Just like "snap," people hear it, and, begin to use it in their own peer-recognizable ways, for their own agendas, and to post video responses. Unlike "snap," we can watch this process unfold through YouTube. "Yes We Can" comes to function differently to different people, easily recontextualized in an enormous range of repertoires, and incorporated into those repertoires through repeated viewing, commenting and recirculation.

Similarly, Soulja Boy: His song and dance circulates on YouTube, people find it, share it with their friends, recontextualize it in their own repertoire—MIT scientists in lab coats, Folger's factory workers, cereal lovers. It is now an element of a repertoire that may be highly differentiated from the original source. In both of these cases, a single message gets disseminated widely, interest groups and peer groups select distinctive features of that message and recontextualize them within their own repertoire, leading to massive uptake of diverse elements of a message. All traceable via YouTube.

Widely circulating media are always resources for locally functional individual communicative repertoires. Across the U.S., countless 12-year-olds say "snap!" or have hair that looks uncannily Justin Bieber-like. Even the ways people walk or gesture or punctuate their speech often emerge from widely circulated popular sources. Features like these are much more unconsciously incorporated into an individual's communicative repertoire than explicit references to "Justin Bieber" or "Jay-Z," but they can be as effective at selecting a group of people who share common ground (and excluding others who might not).

Due to digital media, semiotic forms circulate much more widely and rapidly than ever. Thanks to digital media, we also have new ways of exploring how widely circulating forms are incorporated into local repertoires. I have illustrated how mass-mediated repertoire elements recirculate and combine in ways that potentially foster not homogenization, but more diverse forms of recognition globally. Individuals never produce exact replicas of popular cultural performances but, rather, hybrid forms compiled of diversely recognizable repertoire elements. Thus, common ground with respect to mass-mediated culture is not found through homogenization, but through new combinations that potentially foster repertoire overlap.

Far from homogeneous, today's classrooms and many urban spaces (Anderson, 2011) are probably more heterogeneous than they have ever been. How do we understand interaction in these heterogeneous contexts? Invoking either essentializing generalizations about how certain groups of people communicate or interactional generalizations about how communication works is likely to be misleading. However, examining how these individuals in groups—students, teachers, political movements—use hybrid combinations of widely circulating media elements may help us analyze communication in even the most heterogeneous contexts. I have proposed a methodology for analyzing how widely circulating media elements become part of individuals' communicative repertoires. In any given social context, looking at how participants draw on mass-mediated semiotic forms in their daily interaction makes it clear that communication involves a huge range of resources, a prime font of which is the internet and digital media. Exploring these repertoire sources and possibilities for overlap across massively diverse individuals provides a way of understanding difference—as well as how to bridge differences.

In the next chapter, *Storytelling repertoires*, we will look at common storylines in YouTube videos, and continue to reveal how internet-circulated resources communicate across difference, form alliances, and both highlight and bridge differences.

Notes

1 This chapter is adapted from a previously published article (Rymes, 2012).
2 James Gee (2007) has documented similar positive forms of participatory culture that emerge from playing video games with names like "World of Warcraft," "Dark Forces of Evil and Cruelty," or "Endless Doom."
3 http://www.youtube.com/watch?v=8UFIYGkROII (accessed 1/30/10).
4 http://www.youtube.com/watch?v=z8_lw3gxOV4&feature=related (accessed 1/30/10).
5 The original Bambi version now been removed from YouTube, but when accessed in 11/15/08, it had received over 1 million hits. A pirated copy of this is still on YouTube http://www.youtube.com/watch?v=D6MUEJtTpLM (accessed 2/1/10). Most commentary on this version is about what a bad copy it is and how it is not right to steal other videos.
6 See the YouTube Cap'n Crunch version at this address http://www.youtube.com/watch?v=gLpncqTpRAE (accessed 2/14/2010).
7 Access the will i. am song at this YouTube site: http://www.youtube.com/watch?v=jjXyqcx-mYY (accessed 2/17/10).
8 To access Muldaur's "Yes We Can" recontextualization on YouTube, go to http://www.youtube.com/watch?v=ZLVXxGMG3Fw (accessed 2/17/10).
9 To access Barrackapella's recontextualization of "Yes We Can" on YouTube, go to http://www.youtube.com/watch?v=l07COcgwmXU (accessed 2/17/10).
10 To access the drug legalization recontextualization of "Yes We Can" on YouTube, go to http://www.youtube.com/watch?v=C0mEDE_w1xo&feature=related (accessed 2/17/10).
11 To access "No You Can't!" go to http://www.youtube.com/watch?v=EUKINg8DCUo (accessed 2/17/10).
12 To access *Bob the Builder* recontextualization of "Yes We Can" on YouTube, go to http://www.youtube.com/watch?v=FNXytgKiAHQ (accessed 2/17/10).

5

STORYTELLING REPERTOIRES

Like the languages we choose to use, our pronunciation of street names, or the way we emulate a pop star, how we tell stories is a critical component of our communicative repertoire. This chapter uses the medium of YouTube and the approach used in the last chapter as a way of investigating how storylines and story elements circulate and change as they become absorbed into individuals' repertoires and recognized among different social groups. We will look not only at how storytelling is a crucial tool for negotiating across repertoires, but also at how non-reflective uses of story elements can lead to strange and confusing encounters.

A great deal has been written about ordinary conversational narrative, and much of that work analyzes how narratives are co-constructed between people talking to each other. That is, in conversation, narratives are not unilaterally delivered. Instead, just as the writer of a popular novel is mindful of how a reader will respond to her words, a conversational storyteller tailors her story to the reactions—be it gasps of astonishment or yawns of boredom—of her listeners. As Ochs and Capps (2001) illustrate in their book, *Living Narrative*, balancing the desire to tell one's "own" story with the need to make it understandable for an audience is a central dilemma of every storyteller. How can we, as ordinary narrators, express our own inevitably deeply complicated and uniquely individual lives in a necessarily abbreviated form that others will identify with? To put it more bluntly: While we might find our own stories fascinating in all their complicated nuance, others might not. So how do we keep others engaged? One way of managing this dilemma is by organizing our experiences into common, recognizable plots and embellishing those plots with recognizable story elements.

And here is where YouTube comes in. In the last chapter, we saw how YouTube circulates emblems of culture—dance steps, clothing styles, or phrases like "yes we can"—which become resources to be deployed in varied ways according to the social milieu into which they are absorbed. In this chapter, we will see that YouTube is also a modern-day repository of video storytelling. Like everyday storytelling, super-viral YouTube videos are compelling to listeners and viewers, in part because they have recognizable story trajectories and common, recycled genre elements. For digital-age people, these mass-mediated fragments of culture have become vital elements of our communicative repertoires.

Stock Material Versus Originality

Another way of thinking about the narrator's dilemma—the need to balance individual experiences with recognizable storylines—is to think of the tension between stock, recirculated material (such as memorable lines and phrases) and the act of creative recycling, or *recontextualization*. As discussed in Chapter 4, the massive media machine of YouTube churns out memorable phrases like "yes we can," as well as dance steps, ways of talking, acting, dressing or speaking. As we will see in this chapter, YouTube also recirculates common storylines. These recognizable story trajectories function in YouTube as pre-formed scaffolds. Into these storylines, an author can recontextualize new storylines, new elements, new flourishes; and the juxtaposition of these new elements with the recognizable storyline has the potential to create new stories, individually spiced. Just as recirculation of Obama's "yes we can" led to myriad different messages, recirculation of stock storylines leads to myriad story effects—not generic replicas. Paradoxically (and in keeping with our Diversity Principle), recirculating stock storylines does not often result in generic replication or copying. Instead, the digital circulation of these elements makes it possible to create stories that convey a massive diversity of messages.

Morphology of a Videotale

Just as Propp's classic *Morphology of the Folktale* (1968) illuminated some repeated formulae or genres of folktales that people find compelling, modern-day storytellers call on formulae to create stories that engage their audience. We look forward to rising action, a climax, a consequence and a resolution in novels we read, stories we listen to, movies we watch. We also construct our own conversational narratives loosely around expectations like these. And, a brief review of YouTube narratives reveals some common storylines there too. In the YouTube story world, one recognizable plot is that of an everyday journey that involves waking up in the morning, getting together with friends, getting food—often by visiting a convenience store, walking down the street, and driving or riding in a car at some point. The story ends when the film fades into reverie or the protagonist arrives at some presumed destination, often vague.

Digitally Mediated Story Trajectories: Two Examples

Figure 5.1 illustrates, in still images, how this digitally mediated narrative plot functions in two super-viral video narratives. (The reader can look to YouTube for the full-length action versions of these video narratives.) The first video, *Lazy Sunday*, is arguably the first super-viral YouTube video posting (in 2005). This video was originally produced in a pre-YouTube age, as a Saturday night live video skit by Adam Samberg and Chris Parnell. (Since this explosive debut, Samberg and Parnell have continued to produce YouTube videos, now as the comic duo "Lonely Island.") The prototype narrative trajectory can be seen in all its ironic glory in "Lazy Sunday." First, Samberg wakes up in the youthy bedroom, and calls his friend, Parnell, to get together; next they head to the convenience store for movie snacks; this is followed by a taxi ride; and, throughout, there are scenes of the two friends walking down the street; ultimately, they make it to the matinee of *The Chronicles of Narnia*, their epic destination.

The last column in Figure 5.1 encapsulates a more recent super-viral video, *Friday!*, by Rebecca Black, which was produced (in 2011) by a vanity music video production company, whose services were purchased as a gift by Rebecca Black's parents. While vastly different from *Lazy Sunday* in other ways, *Friday!* illustrates the same prototypical story elements: First, she wakes up and gets food. (We never actually see her eating, but she talks about it: "Gotta get my bowl, gotta have cereal.") Next, she finds friends and rides in a car. In addition to Rebecca riding with her own friends in a car, in the middle of the video, the car ride element repeats as a bonus, hip hop, rapping car ride, in which the protagonist (Rebecca Black, party-girl) is bizarrely absent, but the African American gentleman driving the car claims to be Rebecca Black (See Figure 5.2). Finally, she goes walking down a street while friends all converge in a Friday night, partyin' reverie.

Additional Repertoire Elements

As the obligatory car ride above illustrates, not only do YouTube narratives share a common storyline, they also share discrete, generic flourishes. Each of these videos embellishes the plot along the way with recognizable story enhancements in addition to the obligatory car ride (see Figure 5.3). These include strobe-like video effects, printed words in distinctive fonts that flash on the screen, emblematic "African American" speech tokens, as in the iconic "copula deletion" in Samberg and Parnell's "tru dat" (when they agree about Google maps) or Black's, "we so excited," or choice hip hop vocabulary like positive "ill," when Samberg and Parnell proclaim, "movie trivia's the illest." Another stock element is hip hop tough-guy posturing—Rebecca Black's bonus car ride scene, for example, and Samberg and Parnell's gangsterish hand gestures, tough-guy swagger and bleeped out profanity throughout Lazy Sunday.

VIDEO ELEMENT	LAZY SUNDAY (2005)	FRIDAY! (2011)
1. Wake up in a youthy bedroom		
2. Get together with friend(s)		
3. Visit a convenience store and/or get food		"Gotta get my bowl, gotta have cereal."
4. Drive in a car		
5. Walk down a street		
6. Dissolve into fun/reverie/vague destination		

FIGURE 5.1   Morphology of a Videotale with Two Examples

VIDEO ELEMENT	Morning Ride to School	Night Ride to Party	African American Man in Car
Obligatory Car Ride			

FIGURE 5.2 Car Rides in Rebecca Black's Video

Story elements like these do not necessarily have static or predictable effects when they are released into the massively proliferating YouTube story sphere. Just as the elements in Obama's speech or Soulja Boy's dance become newly functional when re-embedded in new contexts (see Chapter 4), these story elements too, can mean very differently when recombined with other features of a YouTube storyteller's repertoire. As we saw in Chapter 4, "Yes We Can" can serve as a message about women's rights, gay marriage, or legalizing marijuana. A Soulja Boy dance tune can be seen as "hip hop" (very bad hip hop), a bonding move among middle-schoolers, or a morale booster at the Folger's Coffee factory. The efficacy of these signs depends on how they are combined with other repertoire elements. Similarly, stock YouTube storylines and flourishes do not lead an isolated formal existence, but are called on to serve infinite possible messages, depending on what other repertoire elements occur in combination with the predictable scaffold.

Stories Must Be About Something: Replication Versus Recontextualization

As stated at the beginning of this chapter, the point of telling stories is not simply to repeat stock storylines again and again, but to be a recognizable vessel for something new, complex, or hard to get across in another way. With a recognizable form—a stock storyline, for example—we can keep people's attention and relay something important and even complicated. However, the point of the story is to contain *something*. A stock storyline, all on its own, is not compelling—it needs to carry something new. Recall from Chapter 4, that those YouTube videos that attempt to replicate, precisely, the original are most likely to be criticized as lame or drift into obscurity. However, when new versions juxtapose the original with another image—Folgers Coffee, for example—they provide a special jolt. Suddenly, "Soulja Boy" appeals to a new group. Similarly with storylines. As individuals, we want to communicate something unique about our experiences, but we need the recognizable storyline to get this across. The stock storyline itself is not intrinsically valuable. What it *recontextualizes* is what matters.

VIDEO ELEMENT	LAZY SUNDAY (2005)	FRIDAY! (2011)
Obligatory car ride		
Strobe like video effects		
Distinctive fonts flashing on screen		
Hip Hop Grammar (e.g. copula deletion; word choice)	"Tru dat" "movie trivia's the illest"	We so excited!
Tough Guy attitude		

FIGURE 5.3 Stock Story Enhancements

Let us think through what this means for the two YouTube story examples we have examined so far. Both *Lazy Sunday* and *Friday!* share several stock story enhancements as well as nearly identical plot structures. However, *Lazy Sunday*'s creators use that plot structure and those enhancements as vessels for their own ironic lifestyle display. *Friday!*, on the other hand, exists primarily as the vessel. There is no story that Rebecca Black has to tell, other than the generic YouTube story that will feature her as protagonist.

Recontextualization: Storyline for Something Else

"Lazy Sunday," achieves maximum irony largely by juxtaposing the cozy nerd cultural elements—such as Google maps, candy and soda, and *The Chronicles of Narnia*—with tough-guy hip hop video elements, such as profanity, urban car rides, hip hop diction and gestures. Combining emblems of tough urban existence with emblems of privileged, white, youthy lifestyle functions as an ironic metacommentary on both youthy privilege and stereotypical urban toughness. Here, each set of emblems functions as a foil for the other, throwing the stereotype of each into relief.

Replication: Storyline Alone

In contrast, Rebecca Black's *Friday!* is not a production she created, but one that her parents purchased from a vanity music video production company. This company draws on stock story elements not to be ironic or intentionally funny, but to make a music video that will be widely recognized as … a music video. In this kind of narrative, "stock" elements are not used in playful combinations to yield ironic metacommentary, but as the substance of the generic narrative. Nor is this stock storyline used to carry some unique story about Rebecca Black, a person who, presumably, has her own biographical trajectory. Rather than creating a narrative that tells her story, or positions her story relative to other stories out there, Rebecca Black's *Friday!* attempts to use these generic story features to be a generic star.

Replication Versus Recontextualization: Two More Examples

To even more explicitly make the distinction between empty storylines, or attempts at replication (like *Friday!*) and storylines as carriers of new meanings, or strategic acts of recontextualization (like *Lazy Sunday*), let us look at two more recent examples of how stock storylines and enhancements are used to carry new meanings.

Recontextualization (Storyline for Something Else): Make Some Noise

While Rebecca Black, an ordinary girl, became fleetingly famous in 2011 by being embedded in a recognizable YouTube music narrative, the Beastie Boys, in their 2012 video *Make Some Noise*, invert this embedding. Like *Lazy Sunday* and *Friday!*, *Make Some Noise* draws on the same stock, ordinary story elements, but the ordinary Beastie Boy protagonists—and every other generic figure in the video—are all replaced with movie stars.

To familiarize readers who might not be familiar with the original Beastie Boys, Figure 5.4 depicts them in their original 1987 video *Fight for your Right to Party*.

FIGURE 5.4 The Original Beastie Boys in *Fight for Your Right to Party*

In the Beastie Boys' music video, *Make Some Noise*, produced 15 years later, they use the stock YouTube video storyline and other common story enhancements but they embed caricatures of their pre-YouTube selves, adding the twist of using real movie stars as the perpetrators of those beastly deeds, and scattering other emblems of movie trivia throughout the video. Still, at the surface level, as illustrated in Figure 5.5, the video narrative, like *Friday!* and *Lazy Sunday*, follows the same narrative plot trajectory.

In *Make Some Noise*, movie stars, posing as ordinary Beastie Boys, go through the typical YouTube narrative. They wake up and head out in the morning (post-party), stumbling down the stairs; then they visit the convenience store; they ride in a car; they walk down the street; and, finally, they dissolve into a confrontation with duplicate Beastie Boys—actually played by other movie stars—who arrive in a DeLorean. *Make Some Noise* metacomments continually on the formal narrative conventions by juxtaposing those conventional elements with typical Beastie Boy antics (stumbling out of the bedroom in a cloud of illicit-looking smoke, breaking in to the convenience store to get beer, hitting on women in the car) and by having the generic story template enacted by already fantastically famous actors. The Beastie Boys' video, *Make Some Noise*, exemplifies how even as standard storylines and stock stylistic flourishes get recycled, they need not be repeated in rote format, in some form of "McDonaldization." Rather, these elements provide a scaffold for creative recontextualization.

VIDEO ELEMENT	MAKE SOME NOISE (2011)	COLLEGE LIFE (2011)
1. Wake up in a youthy bedroom		
2. Get together with friend(s)		
3. Visit a convenience store and/or get food		
4. Drive in a car		No driving on campus…
5. Walk down a street		
6. Dissolve into fun/reverie/vague destination		

FIGURE 5.5 Morphology of a Videotale with Two More Examples

Replication (Storyline Alone): YouTube University

In contrast to *Make Some Noise*, there are much more common and simpler YouTube videos that draw on the youthy feel of the stock YouTube narrative elements to serve more one-dimensional self-promotional goals. These videos do resonate with a "McDonaldization" feel. Rather than strategically recontextualizing new elements in the stock storyline, providing a foil for these stock features, these videos feature these stock elements as if they could stand on their own as something substantive. Just as Rebecca Black's video was meant to use the entire stock format and elements to stand on their own as a representation of Rebecca Black, other commercial ventures attempt to reproduce stock video formats to promote themselves. However, self-promotion is difficult when whatever is being promoted is largely absent and only the stock story elements remain.

Some universities, for example, have their own YouTube sites, where they are continually posting "ordinary" (yet promotional) videos about student life. One university's video about campus life, for example (see the last column in Figure 5.5), reproduces many of the common video narrative repertoire elements: The video opens with one young man reading on a bench, during morning classes; he then meets up with a friend; visits a convenience store; they walk the streets of university city in typical stop-action video style; and, they dissolve into a general array of campus iconography. (There is no car ride, but then cars are not really part of the campus life at this urban university.)

In a very simple form, this video calls on common YouTube narrative elements, adding a casual and arguably hip aura to an overall wholesome portrayal of the prospect of campus living. However, like the Rebecca Black video, while it reproduces these stock storylines, nothing new is recontextualized within it. Just as Rebecca Black's video is neither a story "about" Rebecca Black in any substantive way nor a parody of any of the generic forms it uses, this *Campus Life* video is neither substantively "about" something new—life on campus—nor is it commenting on the generic elements it invokes in a new creative way.

As these four examples begin to illustrate, while metacommentary may be the order of the day on YouTube (where heavy irony and parody reign), there are cases where the use of stock narrative elements occurs with limited awareness of the relationship of these stock elements to the message they want to convey. One might think that unreflective use of stock story elements would be the "safe" option—it might be boring, but at least it is not risky. However, precisely the lack of awareness that fuels rote replication can cause such reproductions to have unpredicted effects. For example, while Rebecca Black's *Friday!* probably seemed a tame, generic video representation to Rebecca Black and her family, likely to spawn generic compliments, instead, the YouTube release of *Friday!* generated sudden infamy as well as fame, largely because of the new ways it was recontextualized in countless parodies that followed. The *Campus Life* video also takes the seemingly "safe" route. It has a general tone of "cuteness" that suggests some awareness of the ironic juxtaposition of stock YouTube narrative elements with Average College Guy elements. However, it also risks leaning too heavily on the YouTube format, minimizing the substance of university life. Instead of being lampooned, like *Friday!*, however, it simply drifted into web obscurity, hardly functioning as a promotional tool for college housing.

The tension between stock elements and the context (or lack of context) into which they are being embedded, points to a more general tension discussed at the beginning of this chapter. How do we tell our narratives in ways that can be understood generally, while staying true to our own story—or the semiotic means that construct our own lives? When merging repertoires, how do we create a meaningful and expansive hybridity, rather than a simple imitation, even a possibly offensive one? How do we accomplish repertoire "crossing" (Rampton, 1995) while maintaining the integrity of our narrative? Importing an African American male in a car into Rebecca Black's music video brought in a stock narrative element, and the awkward use of the iconic "habitual be" of some forms of African American English ("I be Rebecca Black") gave a repertoire nod toward hip hop, but, unlike Samberg and Parnell's video, nothing new was recontextualized in the usual narrative. Rather, stock stylistic elements were simply reproduced, tossed in, transparently imitative.

Fortunately, for the general YouTube cultural well-being, and life in general, even the most crass imitations do not doom us to "McDonaldization." In the face of even the worst imitations, still, the *Diversity Principle* is in play: Rebecca Black's *Friday!*, like Soulja Boy's dance (see Chapter 4), engendered a new generation of parodies. One particularly heterogeneous new mixture aired on the Jimmy Fallon Late Night show, and potentially breathed life into Black's imitative videotale. When Jimmy Fallon's parody included Stephen Colbert, the Roots, and a handful of semi-celebrities and special effects (including the New York Knicks cheerleaders and Taylor Hicks—former American Idol star, fireworks, and a brief appearance by a giant scannable DR code), the narrative blossomed into a highly reflexive repertoire mixture. Its ironic peek occurred when the musician, "Black Thought" of the Roots appeared, in place of the generic African American man, being pushed across stage in a pretend car (see Figure 5.6), ironically transforming the tough "urban" image into a toddlerish play scene.

While images like an African American driving a car, or the use of stereotyped African American speech like "I be Rebecca Black" are widely circulating repertoire elements, when they are deployed with minimal awareness, their effects can be lost on their users and, worse, offensive to their audience. Increasingly, with entextualized digital repertoire elements circulating so widely today, it can be possible to recontextualize images in ways that lead inadvertently to unfortunate effects. For example, one university promotional web page juxtaposed a caption about "green" educational programs in the city's public high schools with a photo of an African American man in a car, strikingly similar to the stock hip hop narrative emblem (See Figure 5.7).

FIGURE 5.6   Black Thought as "Generic Black Driver" in Rebecca Black Parody

LEARNING GREEN

The sustainability workshop is putting 29 high school students to work on solving some of the world's toughest problems. Growing the economy while saving the planet: How's that for a senior project?

FIGURE 5.7   Caption and Photo Promoting Green Education

While this gentleman is being used to illustrate the high school green education project, the image bears an iconic resemblance to the hip hop stand-in male in the Rebecca Black video (subsequently parodied by Black Thought of The Roots). Choosing an image to tell a story about green educational initiatives could probably have been done with more awareness. Here, a "stock" image, being used without any sense of the effects of recontextualization, can lead to unintended meanings. Is this really the best picture available to represent black men in a story about high school education in Philadelphia?

Images continue to recirculate, to appear in new contexts and engender new effects. However, as the three images juxtaposed in Figure 5.8 illustrate, those new versions can be widely divergent, and the impressions they carry are not always forward-looking or creatively generative.

Telling a Story: Matching Image and Substance

What is the real difference between these recontextualizations? Why does the Roots parody seem full of life, an actual celebration of entertainment, while the "green" education rep seems to detract from the story about "green education." This may bring us full circle to the value of storytelling. In his book *Contagious: Why Things Catch On*, Jonah Berger (2013) attempts to explain why some internet stories or videos go "viral" while some do not. One of the keys to going viral, he points out, is telling a good story. But, part of what makes a story good is that the story itself includes the crucial information that you want your audience to remember. Once again, you cannot simply use a stock storyline. It has to carry something for you. To use one of Berger's examples, if you want to sell "Panda" brand cheese by making a viral video tale, it will be helpful to have a panda in your story, but not so helpful to have someone dramatically catching a huge fish, even if that, generically, makes a good story. In other words, YouTube stories that are designed to communicate a certain message, should probably feature something that represents that message. By this same logic, parodies, like the Beastie Boys' parody of themselves, or the Stephen Colbert/Roots version of the Rebecca Black song, can be

Rebecca Black	Black Thought (Roots)	"Green" Education Rep

FIGURE 5.8 Black Man in Car: Full Circle. Dead End?

wildly successful, because they are clearly about the story they are mocking. And, often, their message may simply be a celebration of creative hybridity.

However, featuring a seemingly popular image of a man in a car for a "green education" story runs counter to this logic. It is not going to be popular, it may even tell a different story—confusing and possibly offensive—about urban education. Similarly, including random scenes on campus may not touch on the most substantive elements of college life. The super generic images in the campus life video narrative may do a disservice to the perks of life on campus. It will certainly not go viral as a videotale—while we can all probably think of a few video stories that would match the substance of college life more closely, and that might certainly become viral phenomena. Finally, *Friday!* certainly caught on, became viral, but not because it represented anything about Rebecca Black. Instead, it became a parody of itself, multiplying exponentially across the YouTube space.

Awareness: The Role of Citizen Sociolinguists

The video producers of *Friday!* displayed awareness of stock "video narrative" elements by choosing them to construct a narrative, however, they were not concerned with creating a narrative *about* something. Rebecca Black became a dupe in their game then, believing herself to be the protagonist of the video, when in fact, the form itself became the real star. This vacuum in awareness, rather than making Rebecca Black's story known, made her seem ridiculous—and led to countless humiliating parodies. In keeping with the Diversity Principle, attempts at simple imitation and replication of storylines seem to be the most marked and least acceptable form of circulation of these repertoire elements. While rote reproduction is easy via digital technology, it carries little value. However, the facility for reproduction afforded by YouTube also paradoxically fosters creativity by facilitating recontextualization, hybridity, and associated metacommentary.

In contrast to *Friday!*, the best videotales feature the meta-awareness of a citizen sociolinguist. That is, they feature awareness not only of the form of the story and its elements, but also the way those formal elements recontextualize other elements to contribute to a particular message. The best YouTube storytellers act as citizen sociolinguists by calling attention to emblematic story features through their recontextualizations. Hip hop fonts flashing on the screen function as a cliché in *Friday!*, but when used to say "Double True" in "Google"-style fonts, in *Lazy Sunday*, entertaining irony happens (see Figure 5.3).

When social actors recognize the contextual contingencies of varied repertoire elements, like the possible funniness of juxtaposing nerdy Google fonts with hip hop flourishes, we say they are acting with some degree of meta-awareness. In the communicative world of YouTube, such meta-aware use of these repertoire elements is the default. We saw this in Chapter 3, in which YouTube videos produced by citizen sociolinguists explicitly name "How to talk like a Conyo" or

"How to say Philadelphia street names." These videos illustrate the point that, for example, saying "Pashunk" for the street spelled "Passyunk" marks you as a certain type of person. Thus, people who used these pronunciations can do so with some degree of awareness of the kind of person they might appear to be were they to pronounce street names that way (or another way).

In YouTube videotales, performers' level of awareness varies widely, leading to dramatically varying consequences. When performers display awareness of the functional effects of their repertoire choices, YouTube storytellers can function like citizen sociolinguists, illuminating trends in narrative presentation of self by acting them out in creative juxtapositions. In other cases, YouTube storytellers (or anyone calling on generic images and storylines) can be dupes; deploying, pell-mell, the widely circulating flourishes of the day, but with limited knowledge of their communicative effects.

Digital Repertoire and Recontexualization as New Resources for Storytelling

Through sites like YouTube, our communicative repertoire has expanded to include newly common digital media. But old communicative processes—such as narrative and recontextualization—are still the engines that drive digital media circulation. Such use of widely circulating repertoire elements can also lead to forays into problematic communicative territory for the blithely unaware. For those who care to investigate everyday encounters with diversity, this realm provides a new frontier for understanding the vast and varied semiotic underpinnings of culture. In the next chapter, we will continue to investigate encounters with diversity, taking a look at generational differences and similarities by exploring the mass-mediated proliferation of youthy repertoires into the realm of all-ages.

6

YOUTHY REPERTOIRES AND ADULT REPERTOIRES

Enter almost any high school today and you will observe a pastiche of performances of youthy exuberance and immaturity, and of aspiring adulthood and responsibility. The difference between today and 50 years ago is that teachers, as much as the students, are often the ones inhabiting all these roles.

This chapter examines this new proliferation of "youth" repertoire elements among adults—those features of communication that might seem to suggest many people now live adulthood as extended childhood. Countless terms have proliferated describing personae of the eternally youthful, including grups, kidults, adultescents, boomerangers, kippers, Peter Pans, thresholders, yindies, alternayuppies, and playalong parents. What kinds of people do these categories refer to? Where do they come from? What communicative repertoire elements are needed to enact these types? How are they propagated? Drawing on examples from advertising, journalism, authors acting as "citizen sociolinguists," and ordinary interactions in classrooms, I will illustrate some ways this youthy repertoire functions in our everyday encounters with diversity.

Many of these terms are coined by journalists and propagated by advertisers eager to extend the appeal of their products to a wider and wider age range. The variation of terms and definitions expresses the expansive reach of this repertoire turn. The term *grups* (a contraction of the word "grown-ups") was coined by Adam Sternbergh in a (2006) *New York Magazine* article, appropriated from a *Star Trek* episode "in which Captain Kirk et al. land on a planet of children who rule the world, with no adults in sight. The kids call Kirk and the crew, 'grups'." Sternbergh calls today's "grups" the "ascendant breed of grown-ups who are redefining adulthood," and portrays them as hipsters with responsibilities. *Kidults* are a sillier version. But, like grups, they are also often railed against as fomenting the downfall of Western civilization. *Playalong parents* get down and spend "floortime" with their kids, and true playalong parents keep playing even after their kids have fallen asleep.

Each of the categories of youthful adult is slightly different, and their distinctions are constructed largely through consumer goods ranging from clothing, games, food, accessories, entertainment, recreation and books. These consumables are sold via a kid-like register too. A Grup-ish snack, the MOJO bar, for example, deploys a distinctly youth-like register on its packaging (see Figure 6.1). There's the youth-like use of "sweet" in the pun, "Salty never tasted so sweet," the use of spoken register, "so there's this bar, right?" The Valley-girl use of "all about" to introduce the bar's features: "CLIF Mojo is all about getting out there, trying new things, combining new flavors and textures." There's also the vague descriptor, "stuff," and the hippy-ish youth resonance of "dig it" ("Your body will dig it too!").

Sam's Club (see Figure 6.2) appeals to a more "kidult" niche, but also markets kid-like snacks to adults through youth speech like "Ultimate"! (proclaiming, "The Ultimate football party begins with ultimate savings!"). This ad also names different party "types" and the different snack forms they will want to have ready-to-hand. The "critic," for example, "doesn't choose snacks on just taste, but also on how easily they can be thrown at the TV or at other spectators." The Sam's Club ad entextualizes several common rejuvenile tendencies: youth nicknaming and name-calling, the youthful demand for "snacks," and the infantile behavior of throwing snacks at the TV screen.

These ads appeal to and propagate varieties of rejuvenile behavior by using strategic displays of youthyness to sell youthful products to a wider and wider age demographic.

But, even when the product is not inherently youthful (like cheez-its™ from Sam's Club), made-for-adult products can be made more juvenile through the way they are marketed. In a Title 9 Catalog, advertising women's sporty clothing, an ordinary dress is marketed to make you feel like a "tomboy for life." It is made from "soft, stretchy TOMBOY fabric." It also features a "super-secret" credit card pocket. As illustrated in this two page ad (see Figure 6.3), usually youth

SALTY NEVER TASTED SO SWEET ™   NOT YOUR ORDINARY SNACK ™
So there's this bar, right? We call it CLIF Mojo. Folks tell us it's pretty darn good. CLIF Mojo is all about getting out there, trying new things, combining new flavors and textures, and respecting the planet by using as many organic ingredients as possible. And because it's got all sorts of good stuff in it, your body will dig it too. CLIF Mojo. Get some. (Text from MOJO bar wrapper).

FIGURE 6.1   The MOJO Bar, a Grup-ish Snack

FIGURE 6.2   Sam's Club Kidults

FIGURE 6.3   Tomboy for Life

register co-occurs with more recognizable adult behavior. "Meredith," a real person depicted in the Tomboy dress ad, represents this kind of tempered rejuvenile lifestyle. According to the case information about her, printed on the ad page, she is youthful: She wears the "tomboy for life" dress, her favorite sport is "rowing" and to relax she likes to roller disco in the park. But she is also a responsible (salary-earning) adult, holding down a job as "reporter for the *San Francisco Chronicle*" and she has even been nominated twice for a Pulitzer Prize.

As these ads illustrate, youthy repertoire elements that may have initially appeared in overtly kid-like products are recontextualized in adult products and lifestyles, expanding their reach. Old school advertising rules about "market segmentation" no longer seem to apply (Wind & Bell, 2007).

Citizen Sociolinguistic Commentaries on Youthy Communication

Just as YouTube videos have proliferated about "how to Speak like an X ..." journalists and bloggers have widely offered up metacommentaries on what it means to be a "rejuvenile." Many books have been published on the rejuvenile phenomenon and journalists have flocked to cover it. The *New York Times* columnist, David Brooks, even claims he is tired of it, pleading in the *New York Times* (with just a hint of youthy bratiness?), "Can we please get over the hipster parent moment?" And, like the "citizen sociolinguists" discussed in Chapter 3, these metacommenters provide us with important information about how these new youthy ways of communicating function in various contemporary communicative landscapes.

In this chapter (with apologies to Mr. Brooks) I begin by looking at two diametrically opposed metacommentaries—or citizen sociolinguistic takes—on the "rejuvenile" phenomenon: Christopher Noxon's 2006 book, *Rejuvenile*, and Diana West's 2007 book, *The Death of the Grown-Up*. To conclude, I will illustrate how "youthy" repertoire elements permeate everyday encounters with diversity by training our analytic lens on some everyday classroom interactions.

Christopher Noxon himself coined the term "rejuvenile." The thesis of his 2006 book (subtitled, "Kickball, Cartoons, Cupcakes, and the Reinvention of the American Grown-Up") is that in the 21st century, the wisest and the most efficient people are the most rejuvenile. The resonance with "rejuvenate" is intentional. He sees the kidification of adult life as, usually, a healthy injection of creativity and energy into the stereotypic 1950s' adulthood that looked like (to their baby-boomer kids at least) a "death march" of responsibility. But by including cartoons and cupcakes in the subtitle of his book, he also nods to the obvious fact that consumer goods play a large role in fomenting rejuvenile "culture."

Noxon recognizes that acceptable rejuvenile existence involves balancing multiple roles. He gives dozens of examples of the "Neapolitan swirl of identity" (p. 184) that rejuvenile existence affords:

- "Well-educated and accomplished women" may also be "doll ladies," fanatically collecting American Girl™ dolls and accessories.
- "Mild-mannered computer geeks ... hoard resin action figures of their favorite anime superheroes."
- The director of a center on public diplomacy is also a "total *Star Wars* freak."
- "Middle-aged professionals download pop-song ringtones."
- "'You da man,' says the insurance adjuster."
- "'Duh!' agrees the building inspector."

In short, rejuveniles are not *just* kid-like. Rejuveniles also (just like Meredith, the reporter in her Tomboy dress) have more traditionally responsible careers and/or adult roles.

Noxon also sees rejuveniles as a logical product of new economic and social conditions. "A distinct new stage of life has taken shape between adolescence and adulthood," (p. 159) he says. Because people live longer, marry later, and have different kinds of careers, there is more time to develop kid-like passions apart or in addition to the traditional roles of mother, father and provider. Rejuveniles, Noxon says, are also resisting today's ever-accelerating pace—seeking out a child's slowed-down and miniaturized experience of space and time.

Overall, Noxon sees rejuveniles as happily inspired people, offering inspiration to us all. At the end of his book, Noxon even imagines a "Rejuvenile Hall of Fame," filled with people who like to play and have achieved incredible things because of it. This Hall of Fame would include people like Walt Disney (duh!), but also bona fide geniuses such as Albert Einstein and Richard Feynman.

Diana West's book, "The Death of the Grown-up," is not so cheery. The arrival of the "rejuvenile" means, for Diana West, the end of Western civilization. The subtitle of her book is "How America's Arrested Development is Bringing Down Western Civilization" (but the cover art, featuring a jaunty baseball cap hanging on the "D" in "DEATH," also signals the connection between consumer goods and rejuvenilization). West is in fear of the plummeting maturity of our society: "our median age has been rising ever since, *even as the behavioral age of our society has plummeted!*" (p. 12, emphasis in the original). She is very worried about our indecency and abnormality: "Being 'fully alive' in today's culture ... is more directly tied to a tally of one's *ab*normal or *in*decent life experiences" (p. 8, emphasis in the original). All this youthful behavior, she argues, is culminating in a horrifying moral freefall: "We live with a social weightlessness that induces a state of moral freefall or paralysis at any new challenge."

To summarize, Noxon and West characterize rejuveniles very differently: In Noxon's case, the rejuvenile role co-occurs with other character traits like creativity, technical know-how, and a youthfully jubilant energy that will not dissipate, even as one gets older. He recognizes the existence of certain deviant and worrisome rejuvenile tendencies (think Michael Jackson), but discounts them as obviously recognizable aberrations. Not all adults today are rejuveniles, and rejuveniles weigh in along a continuum in the degree to which they manifest rejuvenile tendencies. He often introduces his case study rejuveniles by mentioning their upstanding profession, juxtaposing it with a shockingly kiddish pastime: "My search for answers begins one chilly Saturday afternoon, riding a *giant caterpillar* [at Disneyland] with a *municipal magistrate* from Ohio" (p. 136, emphasis mine).

Diana West, on the other hand, sees the death of the grown-up as a societal phenomenon afflicting all of "us." There is no such thing as hybrid identities for West. We are "society," and we are now ALL perpetual adolescents, delusional victims, soon to fall from our superior position as rulers of the Western world.

Citizen Sociolinguistic Blindspots: Lack of Awareness of Their Own Performance

As should be obvious, these two books have characterized rejuveniles very differently. Noxon likes them. West does not. In their own use of youthy language, however, their texts are not very different. Both are performing the rejuvenile role. Both are using the rejuvenile emblems I mentioned earlier—even West, who claims to despise them.

This is not such a surprise coming from Noxon, who confesses at many points throughout the book, sometimes with a bit of anxiety, that he too is a rejuvenile. In describing his own "formative floundering years" he remarks, "I actually wore a T-shirt printed with the now-cringe-inducing catchphrase *whatever*" (p. 182).

Noxon also freely wields casual, rejuvenile lexicon ("kid" rather than "child"), as in "I got a serious job, got married, had a *kid*, then another" (p. 183).

He joyously enacts the youthful practice of name-calling, coining the term, *Harrumphing Codgers*, which he defines on his blog as "Social critics who see the rejuvenile impulse as destructive, regressive, and quite possibly, a harbinger of the collapse of Western civilization" (e.g., Diana West).

While Noxon's text is just mildly sprinkled with these rejuvenile hooks, West is almost relentlessly rejuvenile in her performance. For example, she indulges in sarcastic, rejuvenile "not" usage while explaining our immature tendency to make too much of a big deal out of Abu Ghraib: She briefly mentions "Lynndie England, the victimizer, whose depredations at Abu Ghraib, of course, make Josef Mengele's experiments at Auschwitz look like the Pillsbury Bake-Off (*not*)" (p. 191). She also uses the youthful lexicon of *grown-up, mom, dad,* and even, *crock,* when she criticizes multiculturalism and "the *crock* that is 'universal values'" (p. 213).

West, like Noxon, invokes "whatever," as in "wasn't the American Male long ago consigned to the ash heap of *whatever?*" (p. 190). And she uses "actually" in a characteristically youthful way, combining it with irony and mockery, as in "once upon a time, the mainstream *actually* regarded *stuff* like duty and honor as dependable anchors" (p. 189). Notice here, also, the youthful use of *stuff.* And, although she does not have a neatly used term analogous to Noxon's "harrumphing codgers," she does her share of name-calling and use of diminutive nicknames, as when she refers to Winston Churchill as "Winnie" (p. 211).

Thus, despite the diametrically opposed *content* of their texts, the *form* of their repertoires is rather similar. Both of these authors are spreading "rejuvenalia" by reusing it to communicate. And, they are both recirculating this youthy repertoire widely, mass-producing it in the form of their books and blogs. West performs the rejuvenile stance even as she condemns it. Noxon both performs the rejuvenile, and explicitly celebrates it. While these metacommentaries on rejuvenalization may convey distinct opinions on the phenomenon, they are, performatively, whether they are aware of it or not, both propagating rejuvenile repertoire.

Youthy repertoire is here to stay. Each day we perform it in a hybrid way. Still, as Noxon and West's books illustrate, using a youthy repertoire does not indicate one and only one thing about the person using it. While Noxon relishes kid-like "play" and uses youthy vocabulary, he also emphasizes his more conservative role of a responsible husband and father. While West also deploys her own youth repertoire, she also conveys arch-conservative attitudes, and Republican nationalistic fervor. By the same token, just because a 40-year-old man has long hair, says "awesome," and plays bass guitar in his garage, this does not mean that he is a "'60s liberal." He may also be an investment banker catering to the richest and most elite clients. He may have had to walk through crowds of "1%" protesters on his way to work.

So, what does this tell us about the "youthy" ways of speaking and acting? These days, using youthy repertoire elements is not a statement in itself. It is—like the use of French, D4 English, a particular pronunciation of "Passyunk Avenue," a stock storyline or Google font—one potential repertoire element, always used in combination with others.

Youthy Repertoires in Action

One might think that in classrooms of all places, teachers would enact the role of responsible adults, using more formal and adult ways of speaking and acting that reflect that role. However, 15 minutes in most high schools will undermine this assumption. In some cases, teachers, pull a "Diana West," talking about traditional values of academic learning, but performing the youthyness of rejuveniles. One teacher I regularly encountered during my research in a Philadelphia area high school, for example, stood outside her door greeting students with youthy high fives and "what up?"s. But, as soon as she entered the classroom, she strictly directed students to put the chairs in rows and get busy. In other cases, teachers, more like Christopher Noxon, more fully inhabit the hybrid role of "rejuvenile," both voicing a youth repertoire and imbuing it with youthy content.

Illustrating this hybrid teaching role, Patsy Duff (2004) has written about how teachers invoke youthy "popular culture" references while in the midst of serious, content-based discussions. In the excerpt below, for example, the teacher mentions the (now dated) TV show, *Ally McBeal* (transcript adapted from Duff, 2004, bolding my own):

Mr. Jones:	Well *you guys* live *like* in the *Ally McBeal* generation, right? Here, the teacher not only refers to popular culture, but also enacts a youthy style throwing in a *you guys* and *like*.

This way of speaking is part of the conversation even before the specific mention of *Ally McBeal*. Up to this point, the teacher had been discussing an article about "cyber ethics" and "internet graffiti." Even while still focused on paraphrasing the article, the teacher has morphed into youthy mode:

Mr. Jones:	((*reading from the newspaper*)) "… some things posted—are very hurtful, hurtful to anyone, but particularly hurtful—to adolescents still trying to figure things out." ((*paraphrasing*)) Then it goes on and says—um—you see that the content of this is the kind of stuff that ends up on bathroom walls but it gets publicized a lot further on the internet plus somehow people ((*more paraphrasing from newspaper*)) …
Sue:	We don't write on bathroom walls anymore.
Mr. Jones:	Plus somehow people still believe more—you know there once was a study done by some people at [a local university] about they wanted to study the quantity and nature of bathroom graffiti male versus female.
Sue:	Way more males?
Teacher:	Way more male.
Male student:	Oh yeah.

Here, as in the *Ally McBeal* excerpt, in contrast to the formality of the written text he is paraphrasing, the teacher's talk begins to contain youthy tokens. In addition, he casually fields banter from the class rather than seizing on right or wrong answers, or even a specific thread for his argument. And, the teacher seems to take a cue from the students, as much as they take a cue from him, as when "way more," here, becomes a measure for the relative quantity of graffiti in men's bathrooms.

Duff's study focuses on how students who were relatively new to English-medium instruction, recently arrived from other countries (about half of those in Mr. Jones' classroom) reacted to specific references to popular cultural titles, names, and characters (like *Ally McBeal*). In her interviews, students who were new to the English-medium classroom largely reported a mixture of being lost during these sorts of discussions. However, they also enjoyed the general feeling of the class and the rapport that such discussions established. Jenny, a focal case study student, voiced general appreciation, not so much for the specific popular culture references, but for the general feel of these conversations. As Duff writes about Jenny:

> What she particularly enjoyed was being able to listen to different people talk and to hear different opinions, "and something really funny will come up." That is, she could observe controlled yet free-flowing discussion among local students without feeling that she had to take a stand herself. Jenny felt that she understood much of the banter, but that some impediments were students speaking quickly, using slang (e.g., she used the example of "that guy sucks") and other unfamiliar expressions.
>
> *(Duff, 2004, p. 259)*

So, while Duff's research focuses on the references to specific popular cultural titles, names, and characters (like *Ally McBeal*), much of the "affectively charged" (Duff, 2004, p. 260) talk surrounding these discussions represents a youthy repertoire, and this repertoire seems to be salient for Jenny. Jenny even explicitly mentions the phrase "that guy sucks" as an example of the kind of talk that escapes her. So, the mentions of popular cultural references merge with the performance of a casual youth banter. While some students may have been mystified by the popular cultural references, they relished the opportunity to expand their own youthy repertoire. And, the "controlled yet free-flowing," character of this discussion was likely due to the mediating presence of a teacher who blended his own adult teacherly repertoire with the youthy exchanges between students. It seems that Mr. Jones was at times talking over the heads of the non-local students, but at other times, facilitating the expansion of their repertoire.

Similar to Mr. Jones class, but across the continent, in Mr. Z's class (the Philadelphia area teacher discussed in Chapters 2 and 3), youthy tokens were often exchanged between students and the teacher, and a casual, shared repertoire developed. However, even as Mr. Z deployed some youthy tokens, he more noticeably merged those expressions with a recognizable adult responsible teacher demeanor and message. In the following example, he brings up some "adolescent" issues (just as Mr. Jones did in Duff's article), after one student, "Rugi" has finished reading aloud and describing a poem she has written and illustrated. Mr. Z takes on an adult tone, to talk about how such "stuff" can be confusing for adolescents, but mediates his adult voice with youthy and more casual repertoire elements:

Rugi: They have been together. They are kissing so that's it.

Mr. Z: Very good. Nice job.

  ((*applause*))

Mr. Z: I like how you started with the idea like "The Truth" right? Like the truth about it. Sometimes we'll talk about teenagers and we won't talk about what really happens and you weren't afraid to bring up things.

Even things like sex and we laugh at that stuff, right? But it is true. Teenagers will start doing that stuff. That's part of—Alim's talking about growing up. You know, you become an adult. When you're 16, 17, 18, 19, your bodies are adult bodies now, alright. And they have adult feelings and that kind of stuff becomes a part of your life, you know=

Cinto: You can have a baby.

Mr. Z: = whether you're doing it or not, right? And have very adult responsibilities. If you know someone who's had a child, you know as a teenager, they have to grow up very, very fast. They need to be responsible for another life. So these are the realities of teenage life so you did a nice job getting a lot of that in there. Good (.) Alright, who would like to go next?

Here, Mr. Z carefully brings up sex and "that stuff," underlining the points Rugi has raised in her poem. For a moment, he even represents himself as sharing their laughter and embarrassment about this topic when he says "we laugh about that stuff." By tempering his more adult repertoire about sex and "adult responsibilities" with the more youthy, "stuff" tokens, he neither lets the topic become silly and laughable, nor drifts into overly adult preachy mode. And, in the next turn, without missing a beat between his serious talk and the logistical business of the class, he seamlessly plays with the others, in youthy repertoire, when they jostle for who will read their poem next:

Mr. Z: Alright, who would like to go next?

Alim: Lynda! ((*Alim playfully volunteers her.*))
          ((*Jorge walks to the podium.*))

Mr. Z: Alright, Jorge beat her ((*claps*)).

Here, he simultaneously jokes about the competition of "who goes next," and asserts his teacherly authority by playfully announcing, "Jorge beat her," efficiently quashing the possibility for a dispute, while being friendly about the game of competition.

Both Mr. Jones' and Mr. Z's classroom included advanced learners of English who spoke other languages at home. However, in Duff's study, these students were in a "mainstream" class, including about 50% local students. In Mr. Z's class, none of the students were considered to be "local" students. As a result, Mr. Z may have been more conscious about tailoring his repertoire to this population. Moreover, because the students were from a range of countries (with slight variations from year-to-year, there would usually be about 15 different countries represented in a class of 20 students), there was a general air of maturity in the room. There was not common shared knowledge of popular cultural iconography off of which Mr. Z could play, the way Mr. Jones did, but still a form of youthy rapport developed. Students were able to listen to each other to create a shared repertoire.

These contrasting classrooms, like the distinction between Christopher Noxon and Diane West's portrayals of rejuvenile repertoires, illustrate how "youthy" talk can function very differently depending on what it is being used to convey. Noxon establishes himself as a bona fide user of youth expressions, a real "rejuvenile," and goes on to praise this form of life. West, however, while disdaining youth behaviors among adults as the "downfall of Western civilization" continues to use youthspeak, perhaps as a way of connecting with her (already fallen?) readers. While both deploy a youthy repertoire, it serves very different purposes, and they display very different levels of awareness as to how it is functioning.

The two teachers here also use youthy repertoire to very different effects. The teacher in Duff's (2004) study, Mr. Jones, seems to use his youth repertoire to depart from his teacher mode and rap informally with the students. He still makes loose connections to the topic at hand, but he also loses many of the "non-local" students in the class, who are not able to keep up with his "affectively charged" talk surrounding popular cultural references. In contrast, Mr. Z seems to use mild forms of youthy talk as a way of connecting to students, while talking about sensitive points, adjusting his talk as one might when speaking to one's children about a touchy topic, to ensure them that you are speaking to them with care and empathy, but also with some knowledge born of a longer lifetime of experience.

Mr. Z has explicitly described his perspective of empathy when reflecting on his teaching values. In a lengthy interview, he described his own awareness of the "youth" perspective and its importance to good teaching. When asked what advice he would give to aspiring teachers, he answered as follows:

> Um, you have to—the first one is I'd always say is you have to remember what it's like to be young. A lot of teachers—like it's easy when you start, but a lot of teachers, five, ten, fifteen years in you just hear them just complain about these kids all the time, and they bring that with them everywhere you know to the break room, into the classroom, and the kids know it, and I just want to be like "were you ever 15?" Like, come on, like that's not interesting what you're talking about.

For Mr. Z, empathizing with kids involves remembering "what it's like to be young." At the time of this interview, he was no longer a "new" teacher. He had been teaching at the same school for over ten years. However, his first advice to teachers is to be aware that what they find interesting may not be at all interesting to the students sitting in their classrooms. Youth repertoire, for Mr. Z, may serve his goal of empathizing with a younger perspective. Even in the interview, he indirectly voices the perspectives of his students: "Like, come on, like that's not interesting what you're talking about."

Like the contrasting books about rejuveniles, these contrasting classroom examples illustrate that youthy repertoire tokens, just like any other repertoire element we have discussed (languages, ways of speaking, intonation and pronunciation, storylines, popular YouTube icons), do not convey singular meanings or functions. Using "stuff" and "like" could mean you are an immature buffoon or a wise and highly articulate role model, depending on how these tokens are used as part of a larger repertoire.

Mr. Z's classroom repertoire also illustrates that the presence of diverse speakers may raise awareness about how one's repertoire is functioning. Because there was not an obviously shared youth repertoire in Mr. Z's class, he seemed to use tokens of youthy banter more carefully than he might have had he been teaching a group of people that shared his repertoire more fully (as perhaps was the case with Mr. Jones). In the chapter that follows, we will see how the presence of "strangers" in this way, and the careful design of discussions and activities that foster multiple repertoires, can function to build common ground, rather than accentuate distinction between groups.

7

EVERYDAY ENCOUNTERS WITH DIVERSITY

You Be Illin'
Run DMC

In the 1980s, Run DMC released the single, "You Be Illin'" and, suddenly, Rap Music was mainstream. Massive numbers of people seemed to recognize the silly encounters the lyric recounted. But, what exactly does it mean to be "illin'?" Back in the 1980s, (when "ill" was still a negative adjective), one "illin'" guy is obviously at a basketball game when he makes the crucial mistake of screaming out "Touch-down!" The rest of the song illuminates other missteps, like ordering a Big Mac at Kentucky Fried Chicken, or breathing Bacardi rum breath all over a girl while asking her to dance. These faux pas are so bad because they are so obvious. But they are also funny to lyricize about because they are layered. The descriptions of each scenario involve not only a spoken punch line, like "Touchdown!" or "Small fries, Big Mac!" but also a set of actions and an entire visual scene that enhance the "illin'" effect. Being "illin'" in the 1980s Run DMC sense, is about misunderstanding language routines and appearing like a cultural alien in the process.

Besides being entertaining, Run DMC's depictions of "illin'" behavior also illuminate the nuances of everyday encounters with diverse forms of expression, and the intricacies of knowledge we deploy to navigate them competently. Chapters 2 and 3 illustrated how multiple languages and the sounds of a single language are candidate repertoire elements—that languages in combinations and the ways we pronounce them or the rhythm and intonation we use can combine to create different kinds of effects. Chapters 4–6 illustrated how mass media, widely circulating storylines, and "rejuvenalia" provide more repertoire elements that produce a wide range of effects. What those effects end up being may have a lot to do with context of the encounter in which they are deployed. Shouting out "touchdown" at a basketball game is, in one sense, a "native-like" use of English vocabulary, pronunciation and stress. But in the middle of a basketball game, after Dr. J shoots a basket, it is communicative incompetence. So, repertoire elements—like multiple languages, stress, intonation, and varieties of pronunciation, mass media iconography or ways of telling stories—become functional (or dysfunctional) in their performance of these sorts of everyday encounters.

However, just as one cannot learn only the textbook grammar of a language and expect to be communicatively competent, one cannot simply learn the rules for the language routines involved in a particular encounter, and assume that it will always operate according to those rules. As anyone who has ever played a game of "kickball" or "capture the flag" in two different neighborhoods knows, the rules of the game emerge differently in different groups. Similarly, every day we have encounters with people who have slightly different repertoires and have acquired slightly different rules for deploying them. Therefore, in this chapter, I provide a brief conceptual overview of how the notion of "encounters" has developed in different fields of study. Then, I will illustrate how classrooms might be designed to help individuals combine elements of their communicative repertoires, often interweaving multiple routines in facile combinations.

In practice, encounters like a basketball game are not so easily distinguished as "everyday" and "institutional," "homelike" or "foreign," "youthy" or "adult," or categorically attached to one "culture" or "language" or another. There are few categorical prescriptions about how one is supposed to use language in such encounters. There are no imperatives speakers follow, like "never scream 'touchdown' at a basketball game," or "always say 'have a nice day' when you are finished paying for your snacks." And blanket statements about language and culture, such as "French is the language of love," are rarely true or useful. Instead, speakers negotiate what works and what does not, and what elements of "culture" are relevant, over the course of an interaction.

From Language Games, Speech Genres, and Encounters to Social Groups

Communicative routines, such as cheering at a basketball game or asking someone to dance, are elements of an individual's communicative repertoire. They are also, themselves, comprised of a flexible combination of repertoire elements like languages, ways of speaking, proper names and cultural references, turns of speech, ways of dressing, and lilts of intonation. Over the last century, philosophers, sociologists, anthropologists, and other theorists of language and communication have attempted to describe and understand how such routines develop, build knowledge, and otherwise function in our lives.

In his philosophical study of language, Ludwig Wittgenstein coined the phrase "language games," to describe these routines and their foundational place in social and intellectual life. Mikhail Bakhtin, literary theorist and language philosopher, used the term "speech genres" in a similar way and specified more closely how emotive effects, like intonation, become meaningful in such routines. Erving Goffman, a sociologist, used the term "encounters" to describe other, less language-focused features of a situation—the number of participants, the organization of the interaction, for example—and the way these features affect communication. Each of these terms, *language games*, *speech genres*, and *encounters*, has added an element of nuance to our current understanding of the participatory nature of interactional routines and their place in a communicative repertoire.

Wittgenstein and Language Games: "The Meaning of a Word Is Its Use in the Language"

Wittgenstein was a rare person who, in the middle of his life and career as a philosopher, decided that what he had written, thought, and taught about up to that point was wrong. He had worked for years creating the *Tractatus Logico-Philosophicus* (originally published in German in 1921), a treatise that was meant to distill language and its functionality into discrete logical principles. But, in midlife, after publishing the *Tractatus*, Wittgenstein's thinking took a radical detour. That new way of thinking is represented in *Philosophical Investigations* (1953 [1973]), a book-length compilation (hereafter PI), posthumously published, of linked aphoristic paragraphs that, in their combination, reject the notion that any meaningful account of human language can be in any way separated from the activities it is meant to accomplish. Words do not describe things. They get their meaning from use. Or, "The meaning of a word is its use in the language" (Wittgenstein, 1953, p. 43).

More specifically, words get their meaning from their role in "language games." Just as words get their meaning from use, activities themselves are talked into being using words. For Wittgenstein, language and use are inseparable parts of the same foundational fabric of social life, language games. This may become even clearer when we look at the list of examples Wittgenstein gave us as candidate language games:

- Giving orders, and obeying them
- Describing the appearance of an object, or giving its measurements
- Constructing an object from a description (a drawing)
- Reporting an event
- Speculating about an event
- Forming and testing a hypothesis
- Presenting the results of an experiment in tables and diagrams
- Making up a story; and reading it
- Play-acting
- Singing catches
- Guessing riddles
- Making a joke; telling it
- Solving a problem in practical arithmetic

- Translating from one language into another
- Asking, thinking, cursing, greeting, praying.

(Wittgenstein, 1953, pp. 11–12, paragraph 3)

By the end of this list, it may seem difficult to conceive of an activity that is *not* a language game. Once we see "thinking" as a language game, it becomes obvious that Wittgenstein is not making a trivial point about jokes or riddles. Language games are the infrastructure of our lives; they guide what we believe about truth and logic, and they affect the concrete events of our lives in the most personal local sense, as when we are greeting each other, and in the most substantial global sense, as when people are reporting events, obeying orders, presenting the results of experiments, or testing an hypothesis.

To make this concept concrete, look at the front page of a big city newspaper on any given day and see what the headlines report. First, the headlines themselves are a language game. But, they are also usually reporting about other language games—and not concrete events: Clinton *threatens* North Korea with sanctions; Romney *refuses* to reveal the locations of all his assets, etc. While sanctions and the hiding of assets are certainly real, physically palpable events, their uniquely human significance comes into being through language games. Diplomacy, politics, and campaigning are all built out of language games.

Now, why is this relevant to an individual's communicative repertoire? Because language games, like other elements of our communicative repertoire, are something we learn over the course of a lifetime, through a variety of interactions; and, whether someone recognizes that we are telling a joke, or giving an order, making up a story or solving a problem, depends on common experiences in doing those activities. Moreover, while doing activities together, people, all of whom have necessarily different language game experiences, use elements of our individual communicative repertoires to negotiate the nature of that language game. Language games are, in a sense, a form of participatory culture, (as discussed in Chapter 1), in which people agree, through participation in activities, on what "language game" is being talked into being.

To use another phrase of Wittgenstein's, we negotiate the "family resemblances" of these activities to arrive at approximations of each others' games: You may have a slightly different way of telling a story than I do, but I recognize what you are doing. Someone who has a general sense of the game of "kickball," can recognize it in another neighborhood, even when the rules are a little different, or the playing field is the middle of the street rather than a green back yard. Similarly, we can recognize a "greeting" even when it is in another language, dialect, or completely non-verbal. Participants learn to recognize the overlap in repertoire elements of each other's language games and in doing so, come to a shared recognition of the activity in progress: You are obviously telling a story, or a joke, or giving me an order. In language games, like participatory culture, the meaning of words and their value comes from agreement in practice, and from the recognition of family resemblances. Participants collaboratively arrive at shared meaning in practice—not from a top-down authoritative reference, such as a dictionary, an etiquette book, or an official language policy; and, as was Wittgenstein's point, not from a set of abstract logical imperatives.

This attention to the everyday participatory nature of meaning was a radical break from the logical positivism of Wittgenstein's old self and of his peers. He explicitly pointed out that much of the abstract theorizing philosophers were doing was simply their own language game—accomplished through their own participatory agreement. By listing the range of everyday activities accomplished through this kind of participatory agreement (rather than discovery of some abstract, top-down logic), Wittgenstein was able to refocus his thinking on what people do with words in the world. Again, "the meaning of the word is its use in language" (Wittgenstein, 1953, p. 43). And, for an individual, this means the meaning of a word is how it is deployed as part of a communicative repertoire in everyday encounters with others, as they negotiate what language game it is a part of.

Bakhtin and Speech Genres: "The Meaning of the Word Pertains to a Particular Actual Reality"

Mikhail Bakhtin, a Russian philosopher and literary theorist, also discussed the communicative routine as a social event, one achieved through interaction, not top-down agreement, and, writing in the 1960s, he called these routines, "speech genres." Like Wittgenstein, he was concerned with how words work in the world. As he writes in his essay, "The problem of speech genres," "the meaning of the word pertains to a particular actual reality, and particular real conditions of speech communication." To understand what Bakhtin means by "particular actual reality," it helps to look at what he considers a speech genre. Interestingly, Bakhtin's list of "speech genres" is conspicuously similar to the list of "language games" in Wittgenstein's *Philosophical Investigations:*

- Short rejoinders of daily dialogue
- Everyday narration
- Writing (in all its various forms)
- The brief standard military command
- The elaborate and detailed order
- The fairly variegated repertoire of business documents
- The diverse world of commentary (in the broad sense of the word: social, political).

(Bakhtin, 1986, p. 60)

This list of "speech genres" maps extensively onto Wittgenstein's list of "language games." While Wittgenstein and Bakhtin are clearly both onto something similar in terms of how language functions, as a literary theorist, Bakhtin was more concerned than Wittgenstein with the emotive, as opposed to the primarily pragmatic, aspects of speech genres. For Bakhtin, the only way to understand words' emotive power was to examine how words worked in the context of a real utterance and a situation, rather than in terms of dictionary definitions or the confines of a grammatically well-formed sentence. Bakhtin would agree that yelling "touchdown!" at Dr. J's basket derives its emotive power not from a dictionary definition of that word, or its placement within a fully formed sentence, but from the "particular actual reality" of the scene within which it is uttered.

In this way, Bakhtin was able to account for how oft-overlooked repertoire elements become meaningful in speech genres. Intonation, for example (as discussed in Chapter 3), is a candidate repertoire element, capable of producing communicative effects. Bakhtin illustrates more precisely how, within the concept of "speech genre," intonation gains expressive force. Bakhtin pointed out that "expressive intonation," is unable to be accounted for in a description of language that focuses only on linguistic meaning, but becomes a distinctive feature of "evaluative speech genres that express praise, approval, rapture, reproof or abuse: 'Excellent!' 'Good for you!' 'Charming!' 'Shame!' 'Revolting!' 'Blockhead!' and so forth" (Bakhtin, 1986, p. 85).

And, Bakhtin explains that the expressive power of intonation belongs not to the word, but to the utterance—that is, the word in context, as it is used within a speech genre. This applies to classroom interactions. Recall the "affectively charged" nature of current events talk discussed in Patsy Duff's research (see Chapter 6).

Mr. Jones:	they wanted to study the quantity and nature of bathroom graffiti male versus female.
Sue:	*Way more males?*
Teacher:	*Way more male.*
Male student:	*Oh yeah.*

From a Bakhtinian, speech genre perspective, "Way more" gets its affective charge not from its stand alone quality as a phrase: "Way more male" on its own is interactionally vacuous. And it certainly is not the most precise way of characterizing the findings of the study the teacher is paraphrasing. Rather, it gains its affective charge from its position in the interactional sequence—repeating Sue's predicted outcome—and a recognizable "speech genre"—sharing predictable information about what goes on in gender comparison studies. The male students additional "Oh yeah," seems to add to this effect.

As Bakhtin points out, and this interaction illustrates, words gain their meaning from their place in a speech genre, not from a static, discrete dictionary definition. Certainly there are limits on what something can mean, but these are based on our expectations for "speech genres," developed over a lifetime of interactions, not on a set of rules for linguistic well-formedness. So, from a Bakhtinian perspective, it is not surprising that the non-local students felt lost in these current events discussions. It was not simply because they did not know the specific *Ally McBeal* reference, but because they likely were not able to follow the affective charge layered into the speech genre that we might label, "sharing predictable gender comparisons." Furthermore, this kind of banter is pleasurable for those familiar with the speech genres in play. For that reason, individuals, even teachers, might end up excluding "non-locals" who may not be so familiar with that speech genre, just to stay in their own familiar and pleasurable banter zone.

The delicacy of negotiating different ways of speaking in a classroom—the rapid shifts between academic content and youthy banter, for example—is consistent with another point Bakhtin emphasizes: Communicating effectively within a language means that one must command a *repertoire* of genres. As he writes, without a wide-ranging command of a repertoire of genres, one can be found "illin'" on occasion:

> Frequently a person who has an excellent command of speech in some areas
> of cultural communication, who is able to read a scholarly paper or engage
> in a scholarly discussion, who speaks very well on social questions, is silent
> or very awkward in social conversation.
>
> *(Bakhtin, 1986, p. 80)*

This seems to describe precisely the difficulties the "non-local" students had during current events talk in Duff's study.

While Wittgenstein identified the importance of the "language game" as a social and intellectual infrastructure, Bakhtin's concept of "speech genre" added the role of the uniquely expressive individual: Inevitably some individuals are well-versed in some and not other speech genres, and this has an effect on the way they participate in the world. And, as he put it, "The better our command of genres, the more freely we employ them, the more fully and clearly we reveal out own individuality in them" (p. 80). Paradoxically, however, revealing our individuality always involves taking part in a social routine. Understanding how people communicate and live together, then involves finding out how, in groups, we share our individuality in recognizable ways.

Goffman and Encounters: "A stranger or Two May Have to Be Invited"

Erving Goffman spent his career as a sociologist uncovering how an individual's behavior is shaped by a delicate dance between presentation of self, and the demands of social structures. In his monograph, *Encounters* (1961), Goffman made a distinction between pre-existent *groups* (he called them *little groups*) and face-to-face *encounters* (he also called them *focused gatherings* and *situated activity systems*—"out of desperation rather than by design" (p. 7)). For Goffman, *encounters* are characterized by "participants' maintenance of continuous engrossment in the official focus of activity." He includes:

- Committee meetings
- Public assemblies
- A Conversation
- A Board Game
- A joint task sustained by a close face-to-face circle of contributors

Each of these is a *focused interaction*. Focused attention transforms what otherwise might be vague co-presence into an *encounter*. Just as the words involved in Wittgenstein's language games have meaning only through their "use," and just as Bakhtin's speech genres have meaning and emotive quality only as part of a "particular, actual reality," Goffman's *encounters* can only come into being via face-to-face engagement.

But, departing from Wittgenstein and Bakhtin, Goffman asks a unique, perhaps more sociological question: What is the relationship between *encounters* and *little groups*, such as a faculty department, a family, or a political party? For example, what happens at a "committee meeting" when faculty groups from two different departments are represented; at a "public assembly" when members of two different political parties are present; or, in a "conversation," say, over Thanksgiving dinner, when two family groups come together? Or, building on our classroom examples, what happens when different social groups—let us call them "native English speakers" and "transnational students"—come together in a classroom encounter?

Sometimes, the structure of the encounter and the little groups involved might have little effect on each other. Other times, the presence of different groups within a singular encounter changes them into a new social group; it is possible, that a new, bi-partisan group could emerge out of an initially disciplinarily divided faculty, a politically divided public assembly, or a classroom full of students speaking many different languages. In any case, the presence of people from *different* groups raises the potential that new social groups can emerge from an encounter. As Goffman puts it, when strangers come together, or people form different groups, then the new "locally generated group seems to cast its strongest shadow." Moreover, for Goffman, the emergence of a new group marks an encounter as "effective" (1961, p. 17). So, in an English classroom in which students come from several different language backgrounds, Goffman would predict that the locally formed "English as a lingua franca" group would be the most likely to provide new norms for interaction in that encounter. Certainly this is the case empirically in most schools; even in those with highly linguistically diverse populations, English dominates.

Despite the tendency of the locally formed group to hold sway, the tendency to exclude some groups in this process prevails. The dynamic between a face-to-face *encounter* and the *little groups* within an encounter sheds some insight on how increasingly diverse classrooms, formed of combinations of many different social groups, can remain strangers within a singular *encounter* or, alternatively, generate local group-ness. It is possible that classrooms can sustain themselves as daily encounters, in which the focus is on a learning event. Participating in this encounter involves certain common repertoire elements—and these are the same properties Goffman mentions that distinguish *encounters* from little groups: The ability to illustrate "continuous engrossment in the official focus of activity," the "maintenance of poise," "capacity for non-distractive verbal communication," "adherence to a code regarding giving up and taking over the speaker role," and "allocation of spatial position." An individual's ability to participate in any *encounter* (or language game, or speech genre) draws on repertoire elements we have been discussing throughout this book and the beginning of this chapter—intonation and its emotive effects, the rhythm of an interaction, the expectations for language games and the joint agreements in practice needed to pull them off.

However, class sessions, like other *encounters*, are also necessarily comprised of *little groups*, and can themselves lead to the emergence of a new classroom group, as participants build a shared repertoire of routines out of their unique, individual repertoires. This is especially the case in classrooms comprised primarily of strangers, who have no affiliation to little groups within the class already. For example, a classroom, in which 25 strangers in a United States high school gather, from different countries, speaking different languages can begin as an encounter called "English for English language learners." In this focused encounter, these students originally join together only because they are in class together. But, depending on how effective that encounter is day after day, this group may emerge as its own *little group* that continues to exist and have an identity of its own apart from the classroom gathering. This group grows organically from the encounter, not because it was designated as a social group from institutional or other top-down authority.

Goffman suggested that the presence of strangers can facilitate the transformation of an *encounter* into a *group*: "if a gathering, on its own, is to generate a group … then a stranger or two may have to be invited" (1961, p. 13). Why would strangers' presence have this effect? Because, in the presence of a stranger, one cannot assume a shared repertoire. A teacher, for example, begins his semester with a classroom full of "strangers." They start the first day in an *encounter*, which may involve routine introductions, an "ice-breaker," or other events in which students stay oriented to each other as strangers, but get to know the routine of the encounter. Over the course of a day and a semester, however, the teacher develops a repertoire of techniques for engaging his students in discussion. The students develop a repertoire for interacting with each other and the teacher. If this is an effective teacher, the class itself becomes a social group and not simply a spatially and temporally designated encounter.

By looking at this interface, Goffman's discussion of encounters and social groups explicitly illuminates new ways of thinking of the role of "strangers" in our midst or, to quote the subtitle of this book, our "everyday encounters with diversity." When an *encounter* consists entirely of people who do not know each other, the potential for that encounter to become a social group is high. This is also true of a class comprised of little groups—and most high school classes, even on the first day of school, inevitably are. In a classroom of English language learners, for example, there may be some students who affiliate as "The Liberian Students" or "The Caribbean Guys" or "The Sporty Boys," on the first day of class. But, an effective *encounter* that includes all these groups could lead to the formation of another larger social group. The conditions of the encounter become the criteria for group membership: A class, joined together in an encounter between diverse strangers and little groups on the first day of school, can transform into a social group with solidarity.

Language Games, Speech Genres, Encounters and Social Groups

What is the role of language games and speech genres in the formation of social groups? And why are strangers important? Let us review: Wittgenstein argued that language games, ranging from the mundane greeting to the act of thinking or presenting the results of an experiment are built through language, and we live in the world enacted through these processes. Apart from these activities, the words themselves have no meaning. Bakhtin, using the term "speech genres," illustrated, in addition, that apart from their role in activities—such as language games—words have no emotive quality. Moreover, individuals develop variable facility in different speech genres. One might be a gifted college professor, but a horrible conversationalist at a cocktail party and incapable of making small talk with the mailman. So, individuals have a repertoire of speech genres that help them navigate different speech situations.

Now, Goffman characterized two different kinds of social configurations that might make a difference as to how one's repertoire functions, making a distinction between focused *encounters* and *little groups*. As a participant in an *encounter*, one can remain a stranger to the other participants. But as part of a social group, one has less rigidly structured interactions, looser roles, and freedom to expand one's repertoire rather than remain engrossed in one focal event. In the ideal case, the transformation of a classroom encounter into the solidarity of a classroom group, students and teachers that begin the year as strangers, develop a shared repertoire of routines. What begins as an encounter among strangers, develops the solidarity of a little group.

Encounters are the only way we ever have to engage with strangers. Encounters provide the interactional structure to initially meet up with diversity. A singular encounter, routine and bounded, has the potential to maintain social distance between participants. Strangers at a basketball game, for example, while jointly focused on the sporting event, might never speak to each other or see each other again. Strangers in a classroom encounter could also maintain that distance for an entire academic year. Ideally, however, the shared routines of an encounter can build the solidarity of a new group. Strangers at a basketball game unite as "Lakers fans." Students in a classroom unite as "Our English Class." As participants move from an encounter to becoming a social group, they necessarily augment their repertoire of shared routines, participating in language games they have talked into being. By making the distinction between encounters and small groups, Goffman was able to suggest how groups—such as Lakers fans, or English majors—are developed through what we are now calling *participatory culture* rather than top-down organization principles from nowhere. Just as language games constitute a world, encounters provide the infrastructure through which strangers come together and become social groups.

From Encounters to Groups: Strangers in Action

As illustrated in the previous chapter, lack of a shared repertoire can lead some students to be bystanders to classroom interaction rather than full participants. They may be present when the bell rings every day, as part of the encounter, but they might never become fully part of the "group" that is that classroom community. In Duff's (2004) research, for example, students who were considered "non-locals," those who were relatively new to the English-medium classroom, rarely participated in the "current events" language game, which were often characterized by mentions of specific popular culture names, titles, or characters (like *Allie McBeal*) and the "affectively charged" language that seemed to be a pervasively youthy speech genre. While the non-locals were still present for the "encounter" of the class, their lack of a shared repertoire of references, language games, and emotionally charged talk during these encounters made it difficult for them to ever transition into being part of the group. Even so, as one student commented, she enjoyed hearing the commentary, and perhaps, even while not formally invited to share in that repertoire, she began to familiarize herself with it. Still, the classroom seemed to calcify into two distinct groups, during current events encounters at least—those who engaged with the youth and popular culture laden repertoire during current events discussions, and those who did not. In contrast, in Mr. Z's classroom, as discussed in Chapters 2 and 6, shared repertoire elements seemed to evolve. And, in interviews, he voiced, generally, his concern for building shared understanding among the class.

While these examples illustrate rather ad hoc ways that encounters can transform to groups, or fail to do so, teachers, facilitators and any group leaders may be concerned about developing more strategic ways to transform classroom encounters into sustained groups with a shared repertoire. This can be delicate. As discussed above, encounters tend to morph into groups through organic development, or participatory culture, not through the imposition of a rote way of doing things or a set of rules or norms. As anyone who has participated in negotiations of classroom "group norms" on the first day of school could attest, even this deliberate act of participatory democracy can often seem artificial. And, those momentarily agreed-on "group norms" are often swiftly forgotten, rather than habitually implemented as a shared repertoire of routines. Moreover, as we have seen in previous chapters, often we deploy repertoires of which we have little awareness. Even though we may explicitly agree on a norm such as, "be inclusive of all voices," we might have little awareness of invoking exclusionary repertoires when, for example, we mention "Ally McBeal" or engage in more subtle youthy banter, enjoying the pleasure of affectively charged speech genres.

So, how can we negotiate the dilemma of establishing a "group" with a shared repertoire, while not forcing it to happen? Goffman notes that the presence of a "stranger" can facilitate the development of a group out of an encounter, because suddenly the group is forced to be more aware of those repertoire elements that may not be shared. However, strangers can also be ignored and excluded. Especially in an encounter that contains many little groups, the pleasure of engaging in familiar language games and speech genres may keep individuals in their own familiar repertoires. How can a teacher interactionally shift this momentum? In a classroom like Mr. Z's, how can a "group" develop out of an encounter that includes 20 children from 15 different countries and language backgrounds? How could one, without forcing top-down norms on the group, encourage the group to expand their repertoires to include one another?

Nudging Students From an Encounter to a Group

One way is to develop curriculum that "nudges" students to use their full repertoire range and share it with their peers, not only the teacher. The social psychologists Richard Thaler and Cass Sunstein (2009) have written about the concept of the "nudge" as a way of pushing people into making choices that are in their best interests. Putting healthy choices at eye level in the cafeteria, for example, counts as a "nudge," because it encourages students to pick food that is good for them. And when nudged in this way, most do choose healthy foods, rather than reach a few more inches for the chips. As Thaler and Sunstein have written, "To count as a nudge, the intervention must be easy and cheap to avoid. Nudges are not mandates. Putting the fruit at eye level counts as a nudge. Banning junk food does not" (2009, p. 5). In the cafeteria, eye-level nutritious choices (like fruit instead of chips) encourage students to eat more wisely. In this way, school cafeteria managers can "nudge" students to choose foods that, ultimately, are in their own best interests. "Nudges" not "mandates."

In classrooms, nudges happen when teachers design projects that push students to maximize their learning by feeling personally compelled to take on certain assignments. While top-down mandates at U.S. schools generally communicate the need to focus on one repertoire in the classroom—"academic English"—it is clear that this rarely happens. And, given the multilingual, multicultural nature of schools, when it does happen, it can force many of the students to be excluded from the group formation in classrooms. Moreover, multilingual students' value as the "stranger" at an encounter, capable of expanding everyone's repertoire, is negated. Countering this inertia, Mr. Z started to develop assignments that would nudge students to value and use their multilingual and multimodal repertoires flexibly in the school context. Over the course of a semester, Mr. Z's curricular nudges would transform his classroom from a simple daily "encounter" to a "group" where students learned about one another and developed a shared repertoire.

One example of such a nudge is the "Poetry in Translation" assignment (pictured in Figure 7.1). After selecting a poem *in any language* which they needed to

You should have by now selected a poem or song written in another language and started translating it to English. Your next assignment is to analyze the meaning of the poem or song, and express your ideas about it to others. It will be worth 100 points, and you have three choices of how you can do this.

Please choose ONE of the following ways to present your work:

A. **Written Essay:** In your best formal English, you should write an essay explaining your thoughts about the poem or song. Your essay should include the following:
  1.) Why you selected the poem/song.
  2.) An explanation about who wrote or sung it and anything important or interesting about him/her.
  3.) Any problems you had translating the poem/song, including words that did not have English words to match them and how the sound of the poem changes when translated (think about rhythm, rhyme, alliteration, symbols, etc.).
  4.) Your interpretation of what the poem/song means on a deeper level, such as the theme and message it tries to express.

B. **iMovie Project:** Using the laptops and the iMovie program, you should create a short video explaining your thoughts about the poem or song. Your video should include the following:
  1.) Why you selected the poem/song.
  2.) An explanation about who wrote or sung it and anything important or interesting about him/her.
  3.) Any problems you had translating the poem/song, including words that did not have English words to match them and how the sound of the poem changes when translated (think about rhythm, rhyme, alliteration, symbols, etc.).
  4.) Your interpretation of what the poem/song means on a deeper level, such as the theme and message it tries to express.

C. **Class Presentation:** After organizing your ideas on notecards or writing them out on paper or the computer, you will stand up in front of the class and present your ideas about the poem or song. Your presentation should include the following:
  1.) Why you selected the poem/song.
  2.) An explanation about who wrote or sung it and anything important or interesting about him/her.
  3.) Any problems you had translating the poem/song, including words that did not have English words to match them and how the sound of the poem changes when translated (think about rhythm, rhyme, alliteration, symbols, etc.).
  4.) Your interpretation of what the poem/song means on a deeper level, such as the theme and message it tries to express.

FIGURE 7.1   Poetry in Translation Assignment Sheet

translate and interpret, students could present their analysis as a traditional written essay, create an iMovie on school-provided laptops, or deliver an oral class presentation. Fifteen out of 20 students chose poems originally written in a language other than English. Twelve of those chose to present their translation and interpretation using the iMovie program on the laptops provided in class. These students spent hours creating these movies, and poring over the language and images that would accurately translate and interpret their poem for their classmates.

Just like students who reach for the eye-level nutritious choices, Mr. Z's multilingual, computer-savvy students chose the project that seemed "easiest" and no doubt most enjoyable—that is, least like a typical, academic English Literature assignment. However, while making their iMovie, students spent far more time with the English language than they might have had they written a mediocre traditional essay in English. Moreover, they used multiple modalities (music, images, video) to enhance their poetic interpretation. Finally, they created a final product that communicated not only to the teacher, but also to their multilingual peers. In this way, Mr. Z nudged his students to maximize and supplement their own communicative repertoires as well as the communicative repertoires of the rest of the class.

Communicating Beyond Language

By nudging students into a new sort of language game, Mr. Z facilitated the formation of a group in his classroom. Rather than an encounter, in which all students were focused on Mr. Z and his repertoire, these students developed new routines, ways of speaking, and sharing—communicating—as a group. Interactional routines—rather than top-down categorical designations of social categories—built this classroom from an encounter into a social group. And, in keeping with Goffman's reflections on the value of the "stranger," individual idiosyncracy in Mr. Z's classroom fostered new relationships by keeping students from relying on old standard categories, ways of speaking, acting, or routines for engagement.

Moreover, students were able to create projects that seemed compelling to them and to their peers, and that drew on their own skills. This communicative accomplishment occurred in part via language—the students did have to find a poem and translate it—but much of their process and the final product depended on communicating beyond language. Translating their poems became not only a strictly linguistic project, but an act of interpretation and selection of images online to match those interpretations. Students who had sat shyly for most of the beginning of the semester presented movies about their poems that revealed their passions and interests. In one case, a student from Afghanistan presented a poem that he thought was originally in Pashto, but was, in fact, a Hindi/Urdu song popularized in a Bollywood movie. Another student, from Venezuela, illustrated and translated a song about "hope," including images and video footage that conveyed a message of hope that put a smile on everyone's face in the classroom. These presentations were not directed at the teacher, and the teacher was not the only one interested in their presentation. Just as the class was compelled by their memoir assignment (discussed in Chapter 2) to write more and to learn about each other, these movies made them more interested in the curriculum—in poetry—and in each other. Students were engaging in routines that called on a much fuller repertoire range than that of the typical English literature poetry assignment. As a result, they valued what they had done.

Finally, and perhaps most importantly, this assignment gave Mr. Z's group of students experience communicating across diversity. They were not only communicating with their teacher or some imagined "academic English" speaking audience. They were communicating with their born-and-raised-in-Philadelphia English major teacher, as well as their peers, speakers of at least 15 different languages. This is important not only to the group formation within this classroom but to their future as communicators outside of this classroom. Lately, language educators and researchers have shown that using multilingual resources mindfully in classrooms facilitates the growth of English language proficiency (August & Shanahan, 2007; Collier & Thomas, 2004; Rolstad, Mahoney, & Glass, 2005). Moreover, maintaining proficiency in more than one language facilitates those students' participation in a world outside of school that is rapidly becoming pervasively multilingual (Garcia, 2009). The world is not a place where "academic English" is spoken and understood universally and used to accomplish every one of life's tasks. Rather, the world, including neighborhoods in Philadelphia, looks increasingly more like Mr. Z's classroom. In the Poetry in Translation assignment, students were nudged to call on a communicative repertoire that includes not only multiple languages but, through the web and movie-making software, multiple modalities. They were being prepared, by communicating beyond language, for everyday encounters with diversity.

8

COMMUNICATING BEYOND LANGUAGE

Repertoire and Metacommentary as Methods

As concluded in the previous chapter, kids who are using multiple repertoires in the classroom are best prepared not only to do well in school, but to communicate in an increasingly diverse world. As marketing types will attest, people no longer stay in tightly closed demographic groups: The same person who shops at Target one day, may appear at Saks the next. Similarly, as discussed in Chapter 6, marketers who promote youthy products to adults already know that "youth" repertoires need not only apply to a certain age group: The *grown man* who buys Pokémon™ action figures may also spend hours poring over his stock portfolio. And, for students in Mr. Z's class, "Liberian English," Bollywood jargon, or the techniques for making an iMovie are not repertoire elements that apply only to this particular peer group or the classroom setting. Given the increasing repertoire diversity in the world, limiting one's repertoire to the routines, jargon, and language of an imagined "academic English," might open some doors, but, in isolation, will limit the types of encounters an individual can have with the world.

In the face of all this diversity, however, how do individuals make sense of the world? Three central questions of this book have been: (1) How do we communicate with people without using the usual demographic categories, like language background, to understand what's going on? (2) What do we look for instead? And (3) what methods do we use? By now, the basic answers to these questions should be familiar to the reader: Rather than using demographic categories like language, race, gender, to make judgments or predictions about people, we look at their *communicative repertoire* which includes languages, but many candidate elements beyond language, some of which have been addressed in this book—ways of speaking, media references, rejuvenalia, ways of telling stories, and interactional routines. To investigate communicative repertoire, we need new methods, and I have primarily proposed the investigation of *metacommentary*, often calling on the reportage of *citizen sociolinguists*.

Communicative Repertoire

In the interest of solidifying a communicative repertoire approach to studying "communicating beyond language," let us return to the definition that started this book: A *communicative repertoire* is the collection of ways an individual uses language and other means of communication (gestures, dress, posture, accessories) to function effectively in the multiple communities in which they participate.

There are some critical issues involved in taking a repertoire perspective, and the very first of those, is that "language" in the most formal sense, takes a back seat to other features of an interaction. Below, in the interest of clarity, I list six critical issues involved in taking this perspective when investigating any context of communication:

1 *"Language" is a sub-feature of "communicative repertoire."* Another way of stating this is that our repertoires are multimodal; while language is certainly a prime medium for communicating, as we have seen throughout this book, other modalities—gesture, dance steps, choice of fonts or how we tell stories are also part of our communicative repertoire. And, even when we choose a "language" and use it, rarely is its communicative effect contingent on their formal completeness. As discussed in Chapter 2, speakers of multiple languages use them most communicatively when they deploy them in combination, not in isolation as two monolingualisms. So, while language is an important feature of one's communicative repertoire, it is just one of many repertoire elements we draw on in any interaction to communicate.

2 *Correctness is secondary.* Being "correct"—in the sense of being "correct" on a language test—is secondary to other concerns when communicating. More often, speakers choose elements of their repertoire that they feel will overlap with repertoire elements of the people with whom they are communicating. Sometimes, this means they may use a variety of ways of speaking in a single sentence. While speaking to high school kids in Chicago, Kanye West, says, "I advise you to stay in school," and "I ain't frontin'" in the same breath; while on a campaign stop, President Obama indicates for a Chicago cashier to keep the change first by saying, "You just keep that," then rephrasing the same sentiment, "nah we straight" when the cashier tries to return the change. Alim and Smitherman (2012) call this "style-shifting." I would say that in both cases, this "style-shifting" is motivated by a desire to communicate with the diversity of individuals in these encounters. Mr. West and President Obama (and countless ordinary people every day) engage diverse audiences not by being "correct" according to a textbook standard, or other top-down criteria, but by drawing from various repertoires they command.

3 *Repertoires emerge and recede.* As the discussion of *encounters* in Chapter 6 illustrated, different encounters call for different repertoires. While an "Eagles fan" repertoire may work well at the Football Game, it might not at your wife's baby shower. The vast knowledge of Eagles' lore, an Eagles shirt, even an imitation of the latest amazing play, may be a highly elaborated repertoire that recedes when in a new context. A highly vociferous football fan may become a quiet wallflower at the baby shower, if he does not draw on his "new dad" repertoire and let his football repertoire recede. Similarly, as we saw in Chapter 6, "non-local" students in a classroom might be full participants in the class when the focus is on academic content and the discussion is predictably formal. However, when the teacher switches to a more informal tone during a current events discussion, the relevance of the academic repertoire may recede, and those students who had been confident participants when the classroom talk focused on academic content might become silent. Their content-area academic talk repertoire recedes in a new classroom encounter in which a youthy banter repertoire takes precedence.

4 *Accommodation is not always equitable.* Ideally, as discussed in Chapter 6, in everyday encounters with diversity, individuals stretch their repertoires to find points of overlap. In classrooms, interactionally skilled and sensitive teachers find ways to bridge student repertoires with academic curricular repertoires and serious topics with empathic youth repertoires (as discussed in Chapters 2 and 6). However, most often, certain repertoires are priviledged in an encounter and, those who do not command those repertoires can be rendered voiceless or inaudible: As we also saw in Chapter 6, the pleasure of partaking in youthy banter might have overshadowed the fact that this repertoire was largely inaccessible to the "non-locals" in the class.

5 *Development occurs through growing awareness.* Were we to live very insular and/or privileged lives, interacting with very few people, and sheltering ourselves from the internet or any form of communication outside our immediate social milieu, our awareness of other repertoires might be very limited. In such cases, traversing social boundaries might become difficult. However, these days, such isolation is increasingly difficult to attain. And so, it has become a necessity to develop more wide-ranging repertoires. As discussed in Chapter 6, inviting a stranger to the encounter can help to shift the dominance of certain repertoires. In such cases the "stranger" potentially raises the awareness of the group that they are using a repertoire that may be exclusive. With this awareness comes the potential to develop new repertoires, learning from the "stranger" as the stranger also learns from the group. While there is always the possibility that the stranger's repertoire will be silenced (see critical issue #4, above), awareness of the stranger's presence and accommodations to the stranger's repertoire leads to the development of the group's repertoire range and a chance for the encounter to turn into real group engagement.

6 *Repertoire elements are deployed in disparate hybrid combinations.* Finally, as the previous five principles have illustrated, repertoire elements—be they languages, gestures, media references, clothing or ways of speaking—are not deployed in pure forms. Instead, as highlighted especially in Chapters 4, 5, and 6 on media, storytelling, and rejuvenalia, repertoire elements are constantly being recontextualized. So, a Soulja Boy dance step can be recontextualized in a classroom full of second-graders as part of their "subtly mischievous boy" repertoire, allowing them to bond, while avoiding "disruptive" repertoire that teacher is on the lookout for. While this kind of recontextualization becomes most obvious on YouTube, in face-to-face life as well, hybrid repertoire combinations are the rule, not the exception: Multilingual individuals deploy their languages in combination, not as "double monolingualism" (illustrated as stilted and bizarre in Chapter 2); multi-dialectal people do not use unitary accents or registers, but strategically blend ways of speaking to address diverse audiences (Chapter 3); digital and face-to-face storytellers draw from a range of repertoire elements, and blend them with others to create ironic metacommentary or other effects (Chapter 5). People do not interact with each other as essentialized versions of their communicative selves. Rather, they select elements and creatively recontextualize them—ideally to expand their own repertoires and engage with the world.

It must be said, here, finally, that while a repertoire approach takes us away from the pitfalls of over-reliance on tired demographic categories, that does not mean that features such as someone's race, their gender, class background, or age are not important. Rather, these are also crucial elements of one's repertoire. However, communication will never go well if we make assumptions about what is going on based exclusively on these elements. "She said that because she is a woman/black/old/rich," will never be an accurate statement. Instead, these features operate in concert with other features of one's repertoire. Zeroing in on one feature in isolation will never be interesting or accurate. Moreover, communicating with a broad repertoire range in mind is more likely to lead to some repertoire overlap with one's interlocutor—and more substantive engagement.

New Methods: Candidate Repertoire Elements, Metacommentary, and Citizen Sociolinguists

Everyday encounters with diversity, however, do not always result in repertoire overlap and seamless engagement. In fact, in many institutional settings, individuals band together, creating repertoires that isolate them from one another. Even within a graduate school classroom, pockets of repertoires develop—the PhD students, the international students, the hipsters, the undergrads. In service organizations and any professional setting the same Balkanization threatens the unity of a group or the potential for engagement across diverse backgrounds. As discussed in Chapter 1, this isolation can limit the potential of any group. Instead of developing a participatory culture and forging group affinities, differences can cut off the potential of developing the full potential of a group of people.

Candidate Repertoire Elements

So, in the interest of investigating circulating repertoires within varied contexts, and developing awareness through metacommentary on them, an approach I have illustrated throughout this book is to develop lists of candidate repertoire elements and catalog them—or have students, or other participants catalog them—in your setting. In a high school classroom, for example, you might develop a list of candidate repertoire elements like the one shown in Figure 8.1, and have the students go about collecting and observing them and reporting back.

Communicative feature	Explanation:	Examples in our class
Names/Nicknames	What different names do students and teachers use?	
Popular culture references	What pop cultural icons do students and teachers allude to?	
Gestures	What are some characteristic gestures students and teachers use?	
Turn-taking habits	Is highly overlapping speech common and expected? Are long pauses more the norm?	
Ways of telling stories/Topics of stories	What characteristic ways of telling stories do students and teachers have? What do they talk about?	
Languages and dialects in play	What languages/dialects/intonation patterns are in use? By whom?	
Youthy talk	Do students/teachers/others morph in and out of youthy ways of talking and acting?	
OTHER	What other evidence of diverse communicative repertoires do you observed?	

FIGURE 8.1 Candidate Repertoire Elements in a Classroom: Students as Citizen Sociolinguists

Once we account for possible repertoires circulating in a given context, we can engage, specifically, with the critical issues involved in taking a repertoire approach. While multiple languages may be spoken in the classroom, students need not discount all the other ways of communicating—mass media references, gesture, eye contact, ways of sitting, standing, chewing gum, or glancing at the ceiling. Communication, rather than correctness becomes important here. Once students begin accounting for their own repertoires, it becomes clear that "correct" according to a textbook or test, is only one small element of communicating in a classroom. Instead, as repertoires grow and change over the course of a semester within one classroom, the knowledge fostered in that community can get fore-grounded and placed critically alongside other "correct" forms of standard knowledge. Talking about the range of repertoires in a group raises the potential for awareness and development. Also, it makes it less likely that one repertoire will be tacitly privileged over another.

This sort of list of candidate repertoire elements can be generated in any context, and become more detailed the more familiar one gets with a setting and the more aware one becomes of the different ways of communicating circulating there. These charts function as a simple way of fostering awareness or repertoire elements through metacommentary. As I illustrated in Chapter 4, repertoire elements can be cataloged across YouTube parodies, or in Chapter 5, across video narratives and even promotional websites. This approach can also be applied to understand the fine-grained repertoires that take place in any professional setting. A jury consultant can fine-tune the repertoire elements that lawyers focus on as a judge questions particular jurors. A police officer can hone the elements that go into the fine-grained questioning of a witness or interrogation of a suspect. These are communicatively complex encounters that involve histories of diverse repertoire elements. Such encounters can become dysfunctional when participants tune away the particularities of repertoire diversity and become locked in their own assumptions about communication.

Metacommentary

After compiling a list of repertoire elements in a classroom, research site, or institution, given the infinite variability in play, how do people in interaction—and how do we, as sociolinguists, linguistic ethnographers, or linguistic anthropologists—figure out which of these accumulated details are relevant? How do people in interaction know what count as communicatively relevant elements? By what mechanisms do we measure the relative efficacy of any interactional move? One important mechanism is metacommentary.

Orders of Metacommentary

In any interaction, metacommentary signals an understanding of what a sign means without necessarily arbitrarily systematizing communicative elements, but by pointing to that sign's situated communicative value. Throughout this volume, I have illustrated forms of metacommentary, including explicit comments on the languages people are speaking "Don't speak Spanish," and the way people speak, "'Passyunk' is pronounced 'PASHUNK'," to more implicit comments on their understandability, as when people claim they cannot understand someone's accent or implicit statements of something's relevance, as when a boring YouTube video story drifts into obscurity. As the inclusion of these implicit metacomments suggests, metacommentary permeates any act of communication. Distinguishing between these types of metacommentary can begin to distinguish relevant repertoire elements.

Metapragmatic Discourse and Metapragmatic Function

Silverstein (1993) has used the term "metapragmatic discourse" to describe explicit metacommentary. For example, comments about how language is functioning such as, "That was a mean thing to say," "I wish you would give me more compliments," or "Using 'sir' and 'ma'am' is polite," are, in Silverstein's terms "metapragmatic discourse," because they are calling attention to how utterances are functioning in a particular context. More pathbreakingly, Silverstein also describes the implicit metapragmatics of just about any use of language. While speakers are usually not explicitly drawing attention to how specific linguistic forms or languages are functioning, they signal the function of any communicative act through implicit metapragmatic activity. Rather than saying something like, "That was a mean thing to say," people may act sad or offended; instead of saying, "I wish you would give me more compliments," someone might fish for a compliment by saying something like, "How do I look?"; instead of saying "Using 'sir' and 'ma'am' is polite" people may refuse to answer ("I can't hear you!") until children attach these address terms to their requests. In this way, speakers signal their evaluations through everyday implicit metapragmatic function. The more we investigate the metapragmatics of language, the more apparent it becomes that every utterance—what might seem to be a simple, or even a scientific, description of the world—is saturated with metapragmatic function.

In describing metacommentary here, I include both examples of explicit metapragmatic discourse, and an attempt to tease out examples of more implicit metapragmatic functioning. Moreover, often cases of explicit metapragmatic discourse are also layered with implicit metapragmatic function. Through an analysis of metacommentary, we can go beyond simply observing that students speak "multiple languages," to accounting for their facility with the multiple and nuanced functions languages take on in context, in any language game or speech genre.

At this point, it might be clear to the reader that normative, prescriptive, traditional, top-down talk of code and how it functions is yet another form of metacommentary. Much of the business of language teaching, including textbook publishing, is itself a factory of explicit metapragmatic discourse. But, as the examples throughout this volume have shown, participatory culture foments its own metapragmatic discourse, as well as more subtle processes of metapragmatic functioning, which may be more finely tuned and relevant. This is where citizen sociolinguists come in.

Citizen Sociolinguists

Citizen sociolinguists engage both in "explicit metapragmatic discourse," as when they discuss "how to talk like a Conyo," as well as implicit metapragmatic function, through, for example, nuanced impersonations about what "Conyos" look like and the way they act when they speak that way. Both practices serve us well in the study of communicative repertoire.

While individuals do not always explicitly metacomment on repertoire elements and how they are functioning, there is always implicit metapragmatic negotiation about their function, or when it is okay to say them. This is the case when students choose to answer or not to answer a question, or when teachers signal, through youthy greetings, perhaps, that it is okay to talk like that in their classroom, or, anytime someone impersonates the language of someone else, while layering on other repertoire elements. Often, implicit metacommentary draws attention to the role and relevance of repertoire elements, but it takes much longer, sustained presence in a setting, like a classroom, to interpret implicit metacommentary.

Final Word, For Now

Raising awareness of the massive particularity of repertoire elements can be a first step to solving practical communicative problems, and to engaging across diversity. Rather than relying on categorical rules on what we can or cannot say to whom and when, individuals can hone their awareness of daily encounters with diversity, looking for regularities, while fully appreciating distinction. As individuals, this paves a more interesting pathway through increasingly communicatively diverse lives. As researchers, educators, or applied linguists, documenting the existence and awareness of growing communicative repertoires offers a non-essentializing approach to investigating a communicatively complex world.

REFERENCES

Alim, H. S. & Smitherman, G. (2012). *Articulate while black: Barack Obama, language, and race in the U.S.* Oxford & New York: Oxford University Press.

Anderson, E. (2011). *The cosmopolitan canopy: Race and civility in everyday life.* New York: Norton.

Ashbery, J. (2012). The short answer, *The New Yorker*, October 1, p. 57.

August, D. & Shanahan, T. (Eds.) (2007). *Developing reading and writing in second language learners: Lessons from the national literacy panel on language-minority children and youth.* New York: Routledge.

Bakhtin, M. (1981). Discourse in the novel. In M. Holquist (Ed.), C. Emerson & M. Holquist (Trans.), *The dialogic imagination* (pp. 259–422). Austin, TX: University of Texas Press.

Bakhtin, M. (1986). The problem of speech genres. In M. Holquist & C. Emerson (Eds.), V. McGee (Trans.), *Speech genres and other late essays* (pp. 60–102). Austin, TX: University of Texas Press.

Baldridge, J. (2002). Linguistic and social characteristics of Indian English. *Language in India 2* (2). Retrieved 7/7/2012 from http://www.languageinindia.com/junjul2002/baldridgeindianenglish.html).

Barber, B. R. (2008). *Consumed: How markets corrupt children, infantilize adults, and consume citizens whole.* New York: W. H. Norton.

Baugh, J. (2003). Linguistic profiling. In S. Makoni, G. Smitherman, A. F. Ball & A. K. Spears (Eds.), *Black linguistics: Language, society, and politics in Africa and the Americas* (pp. 155–168). New York & London: Routledge.

Bauman, R. & Briggs, C. (1990). Poetics and performance as critical perspectives on language and social life. *Annual Review of Anthropology 19*: 59–88.

Berger, J. (2013). *Contagious: Why things catch on.* New York: Simon & Schuster.

Black, R.W. (2008). *Adolescents and online fan fiction.* New York: Peter Lang.

Blackledge, A. & Creese, A. (2010). *Multilingualism: A critical perspective.* London & New York: Continuum.

Blommaaert, J. (2008). Language, asylum, and the national order. *Working Papers in Urban Languages and Literacies 50.*

Blommaert, J. (2010). *The sociolinguistics of globalization.* Cambridge University Press.

Brooks, D. (2007). Mosh Pit meets Sandbox, *New York Times*, February 25.

Burgess, J. & Green, J. (2009). *YouTube.* Cambridge, MA: Polity.

Collier, V. & Thomas, W. (2004). The astounding effectiveness of dual language education for all. *NABE Journal of Practice 2*: 1–20.

Creese, A. & Blackledge, A. with Taskin Baraç, Arvind Bhatt, Shahela Hamid, Li Wei, Vally Lytra, Peter Martin, Chao-Jung Wu, & Dilek Yağcioğlu (2011). Separate and flexible bilingualism in complementary schools: Multiple language practices in inter-relationship. *Journal of Pragmatics 43*: 1196–1208.

Crystal, D. (2003). *English as a global language.* Cambridge: Cambridge University Press.

Crystal, D. (2010). *A little book of language.* New Haven: Yale University Press.

Duff, P. (2004). Intertextuality and hybrid discourses: The infusion of pop culture in educational discourse. *Linguistics and Education 14*: 231–276.

Duranti, A. (1994). *From grammar to politics: Linguistic anthropology in a Western Samoan village.* Berkeley: University of California Press.

Duranti, A. & Reynolds, J. (2000). Phological and cultural innovations in the speech of Samoans in Southern California. *Estudios de Sociolingüística 1* (1): 93–110.

Erickson, F. (1996). Going for the zone: The social and cognitive ecology of teacher–student interaction in classroom conversations. In D. Hicks (Ed.), *Discourse, learning, and schooling* (pp. 29–62). New York: Cambridge University Press.

Erickson, F. & Shultz, J. (1982). *The counselor as gatekeeper: Social interaction in interviews.* New York: Academic Press.

Flores, N. (2012). Dynamic lingualism. Paper presented at the *57th Annual Conference of the International Linguistics Association.* New York (April 14).

García, O. (2009). *Bilingual education in the 21st century: A global perspective.* Oxford: Wiley Blackwell.

Gee, J. (2007). *What video games have to teach us about learning and literacy.* New York: Palgrave Macmillan.

Goffman, E. (1961). *Encounters: Two studies in the sociology of interaction.* Indianapolis and New York: The Bobbs-Merrill Company.

Graddol, D. (1997). *The future of English: A guide to forecasting the popularity of English in the 21st century.* London: The British Council.

Graddol, D. (2006). *English next.* London: The British Council.

Grosjean, F. (1985). The bilingual as a competent but specific speaker-hearer. *Journal of Multilingual and Multicultural Development 6*: 467–477.

Grosjean, F. (1995). A psycholinguistic approach to code-switching: The recognition of guest words by bilinguals. In L. Milroy and P. Muysken (Eds.), *One speaker, two languages: Cross-disciplinary perspectives on code-switching.* Cambridge: Cambridge University Press.

Gumperz, J. (1964). Linguistic and social interaction in two communities. *American Anthropologist 66*:6 (part 2): 137–154.

Gumperz, J. (1965). Language. *Biennial Review of Anthropology 4*: 84–120.

Gumperz, J. (1978). Dialect and conversational inference in urban communication. *Language and Society 7*: 393–409.

Gutiérrez, K. & Rogoff, B. (2003). Cultural ways of learning: Individual traits or repertoires of practice. *Educational Researcher 32*, 5: 19–25.

Hayes, E. & Gee, J. (2010). Public pedagogy through videogames: Design, resources, and affinity spaces. In J. A. Sandlin, B. D. Schultz, & J. Burdick (Eds.), *Handbook of public pedagogy: Education and learning beyond schooling* (pp. 185–193). New York: Routledge.

Heller, M. (2006). *Linguistic minorities and modernity: A sociolinguistic ethnography*. London & New York: Continuum.

Howard, K. & Lipinoga, S. (2010). Closing down openings: Pretextuality and misunderstanding in parent-teacher conferences with Mexican immigrant families. *Language and Communication 30*(1): 33–47.

Hutcheon, L. (1994). *Irony's edge: The theory and politics of irony*. London: Routledge.

Jenkins, H. (1992). *Textual poachers: Television fans and participatory culture*. New York: Routledge.

Jenkins, H. (2006). *Fans, bloggers, and gamers: Exploring participatory culture*. New York: New York University Press.

Jørgensen, N. (2008). Polylingual languaging around and among children and adolescents. *International Journal of Multilingualism 5*(3): 161–176.

Labov, W. (1963). The social motivation of a sound change. *Word 19*: 273–309.

Ladson-Billings, G. (2001). *Crossing over to Canaan: The journey of new teachers in diverse classrooms*. San Francisco: Jossey-Bass.

Levy, P. (1997). *Collective intelligence*. New York & London: Plenum.

Locke, John L. (1995). *A child's path to spoken language*. Cambridge: Harvard University Press.

Moore, R. (2011a). Overhearing Ireland: Mediatized personae in Irish accent culture. *Language & Communication 31*: 229–242.

Moore, R. (2011b). "If I actually talked like that, I'd pull a gun on myself": Accent, avoidance, and moral panic in Irish English." *Anthropological Quarterly 84*(1): 41–64.

Mori, K. (1997). *Polite lies: On being a woman caught between cultures*. New York: Ballantine.

Moss, C. (2005). College dropout Kanye tells high school students not to follow in his footsteps. MTV News. Retrieved August 11, 2013 from http://www.mtv.com/news/articles/1517484/kanye-tells-students-stay-school.jhtml.

Noxon, C. (2006). *Rejuvenile: Kickball, cartoons, cupcakes, and the reinvention of the American grown-up*. New York: Crown.

Ochs, E. & Capps, L. (2001). *Living narrative: Creating lives in everyday storytelling*. Cambridge: Harvard University Press.

Propp, V. (1968). *Morphology of the folktale*. Austin: University of Texas Press.

Purnell, T., Isardi, W., & Baugh, J. (1999). Perceptual and phonetic experiments on American English dialect identification. *Journal of Language and Social Psychology 18*: 10–30.

Rampton, B. (1995). *Crossing: Language and ethnicity among adolescents*. London: Longman.

Rampton, B. (2006). *Language in late modernity*. Cambridge & New York: Cambridge University Press.

Rampton, B. (2010). From "multi-ethnic urban heteroglossia" to "contemporary urban vernaculars." *Working Papers in Urban Languages and Literacies 61*.

Reyes, A. (2013). Linguistic hybrids, modern anxieties, and imagined racial figures in the Philippines. *Paper presented at the American Association for Applied Linguistics Annual Conference, Dallas, TX, March 16–19*.

Robb, G. (2007). *The discovery of France: A historical geography*. New York: Norton.

Rolstad, K., Mahoney, K., & Glass, G. (2005). The big picture: A meta-analysis of program effectiveness research on English language learners. *Educational Policy 19*, 572–594.

Rymes, B. (2010). Classroom discourse analysis: A focus on communicative repertoires. In N. Hornberger and S. McKay (Eds.), *Sociolinguistics and language education* (pp. 528–546). Buffalo, NY: Multilingual Matters.

Rymes, B. (2012). Recontextualizing YouTube: From micro-macro to mass-mediated communicative repertoires. *Anthropology & Education Quarterly 43* (2): 214–227.

Rymes, B., Cahnmann-Taylor, M., & Souto-Manning, M. (2008). Bilingual teachers' performances of power and conflict. *Teaching Education Journal 19*(2): 105–119.

Shohamy, E. G. (2007) *Language policy: Hidden agendas and new approaches.* New York: Routledge.

Silverstein, M. (1993). Metapragmatic discourse and metapragmatic function. In J. Lucy (Ed.), *Reflexive language: Reported speech and metapragmatics* (pp. 33–58). New York: Cambridge University Press.

Silverstein, M. & Urban, G. (Eds.) (1996). *Natural histories of discourse.* Chicago: University of Chicago Press.

Sternbergh, A. (2006). Up with grups. *New York Magazine*, April, 2006.

Swinehart, K. (2011). Footing and role alignment online: Andean, indigenous or hip-hop nations? Paper presented as part of the panel, *Tracing Mobile Language Practices Across Digital Territories*, at the *Annual Meeting of the American Anthropological Association*, November, Montreal, CA.

Thaler, R. H. & Sunstein, C. R. (2009). *Nudge: Improving decisions about health, wealth, and happiness.* New York: Penguin.

Tse, L. (2001). *Why don't they learn English? Separating fact from fallacy in the U.S. language debate.* New York: Teachers College Press.

West, D. (2007). *The death of the grown-up: How America's arrested development is bringing down Western civilization.* New York: St. Martin's Press.

Wind, Y. & Bell, C. (2007). Market segmentation. In M. Baker & S. Hart (Eds.), *The Marketing Book* (pp. 222–244). New York: Elsevier.

Wittgenstein, L. (1953). *Philosophical Investigations.* Oxford: Blackwell.

INDEX